THE GNOSIS OF SIMON MAGUS

BY KEITH HILL

CLASSICS OF WORLD MYSTICISM
Psalms of Exile and Return
The Bhagavad Gita A New Poetic Version
I Cannot Live Without You
Selected Poetry of Mirabai and Kabir
Interpretations of Desire
Mystical Love Poems by the Sufi Master Ibn 'Arabi

NON-FICTION
The New Mysticism
The God Revolution
Striving to Be Human
Experimental Spirituality
Practical Spirituality
Psychological Spirituality
What Is Really Going On?
Where Do I Go When I Meditate?
How Did I End Up Here?

FICTION
Puck of the Starways
Blue Kisses

POETRY
The Ecstasy of Cabeza de Vaca
The Lounging Lizard Poet of the Floating World
Out of the Way World Here Comes Humanity!

WITH PETER CALVERT
The Matapaua Conversations
Learning Who You Are
The Kosmic Web

The Gnosis of
Simon Magus

Keith Hill

attar‖books

First published in 2023 by Attar Books
Auckland, New Zealand

Casebook ISBN 978-1-99-115704-1
Paperback ISBN 978-1-99-115703-4

Cover image: Shutterstock

Attar Books is a New Zealand company that explores
contemporary and historical spiritual experiences, culture,
concepts and practices. For more information on Attar Books'
publications visit the website:.

www.attarbooks.com

Contents

Introduction

History declares Simon Magus a necromancer and heretic. The New Testament *Acts* depicts him as a magician who claimed to have extraordinary powers. Supposedly, after his students converted to Christianity, he jealously watched Peter and John pass the Holy Spirit to new converts by the laying of hands during baptism. He then offered the two apostles money to share their power with him. They refused, but the incident gave Simon's name to the sin of simony.

The Church Fathers subsequently wrote of Simon Magus that he was able to perform magic because he was possessed by demons, that he taught false Gnostic doctrines, and that he was accompanied by a former prostitute named Helen. On these grounds the Church Father Epiphanious declared Simon Magus the first heretic.

Simon's death is described as resulting from hubris. The Magus wanted to show off his powers so he challenged the apostle Peter to a series of duels. These culminated in the Magus attempting to ascend to heaven in a chariot made of fire. However, Peter's prayers proved more powerful, bringing the flying Simon crashing to the ground, killing him.

Another story claims that one of Simon's duels with Peter involved the Magus impersonating a man named Faustus. Faustus became a name to conjure with when, in the early 1500s, Johann Georg Faust, a German alchemist and astrologer was, like Simon Magus, denounced as a fraudulent magician and declared a heretic by the Church. Numerous versions of this Faust story followed, most famously the dramatisations of Christopher Marlowe and Johann Wolfgang von Goethe. Marlowe's Faustus is an intellectually hungry scholar who sells his soul to Mephistopheles in exchange for knowledge and power. For his overreach he is condemned to hell. Conversely, in Goethe's play Faustus is saved by his love for Helen. The success of their plays gave Faustus immortality, his story being retold in music, theatre and literature by Franz Liszt, Ivan Turgenev, Thomas Mann, Gertrude Stein, Václav Havel, John Banville and others.

Authors who return the Faustus legend to its roots in Simon Magus number far fewer, but include Dante, who placed Simon Magus in his third hell, Carl Jung, who identified Simon Magus with a spirit guide in *The Red Book*, and Anita Mason in her novel *The Illusionist*. Mason situates Simon Magus in the first century, after the death of Jesus. Giving the key participants Jewish rather than unhistorical Greek names—such as Joshua for Jesus, Kepha for Peter, and Saul for Paul—Mason creates a fictional version of Simon Magus grounded in the historical record. Mason's novel, combined with my own research into Gnostic thought and the origins of Christianity, stimulated the version of Simon Magus' story presented here.

The first issue facing anyone examining Simon Magus' narrative is that the mythologising projected onto it is far too simplistic. The most detailed stories about Simon were written by the Ebionites, an early Christian group who lived from the second and fifth centuries. According to them, Simon Magus was born in Samaria, became a disciple of John the Baptist, and travelled to Alexandria to study Egyptian magic. He subsequently returned to Samaria where he garnered notoriety by performing magic tricks. Eventually, he contended with Simon Peter, who brought down the flying Magus with a prayer. Variations on this story are repeated in the writings of the Church Fathers.

Digging beneath this narrative, two issues become apparent.

The first is that the Ebionites and Church Fathers chose to make Simon Magus a spiritual adversary, who they then 'took out'. Because they began doing so a century after the Magus' death, he either still had a sufficient number of active followers for that effort to be worth making, or they decided he was useful as a symbolic adversary representing all their enemies.

The second issue is that if Simon Magus was connected with John the Baptist, and Simon was a Gnostic heretic, what was John's relationship to Gnostic thought? This question becomes even more complex when further digging reveals that John's clothing, diet, and desert life-style were in keeping with the Nazirs, ascetics who sought to emulate the desert prophets of several centuries before. John subsequently became a foundational figure for the Mandaeans, a Gnostic group that, as a people, still survive today. Add to this the fact that early Christianity's apostle to the Gentiles, Paul of Tarsus, was claimed by the first century Valentinians as a Gnostic forebear, but was viewed by the Ebionites as an enemy, and we begin to see the outline of an alternative history.

Modern scholars began their reappraisal of the interlinked history of Gnosticism and Christianity in 1896, with the discovery of a papyrus codex written in Coptic that contained three Gnostic texts, *The Gospel of Mary*, *Apocryphon of John*, and *The Sophia of Jesus Christ*. These showed that the Church Fathers, when stigmatising the Gnostics, had not represented their teachings either clearly or fairly.

The complex nature of Gnostic thought was further revealed when nearly fifty Gnostic treatises were discovered in 1945 near Nag Hammadi in Egypt. These texts led not only to a re-evaluation of Gnostic teachings, but also of early Christian history and theology. One fundamental point that study of the Nag Hammadi texts makes clear is that collectively the Gnostics—just like first and second century Christians—were never a homogeneous group. Those who identify Gnostics as Christian heretics are over-simplifying. While Christian Gnostics were predominant, other Gnostics were Egyptian, Jewish, Samarian and Zoroastrian in orientation. Ideas that became central to Gnostic thought also pre-existed Christianity, being present in the schools of the Persian Magi and the Greco-Egyptian Hermeticists. This means the Gnostics cannot collectively be characterised as post-Christian. What we know of Simon Magus's thought indicates he drew on Zoroastrian, Jewish and Greco-Egyptian doctrines. Hence a re-evaluation of Simon Magus is overdue. This work is contributes to that task.

One of the fascinating aspects of the first century is that we are dealing as much with mythology as history. Any narrative involving Simon Magus has to critically weigh the legends, all recorded by those who judged him an adversary. My approach here is to combine history and mythology in a way that reflects my own aim of presenting a view sympathetic to Simon Magus, while bringing to life the intense human drama of the period.

This version of Simon Magus's story is set in 52 CE. By that time the Jewish peoples had struggled against occupation for centuries: Rome was merely the latest in a long line of invaders. Jerusalem was consequently an intensely political city. Various religious factions vied for power, while in the countryside Zealots and other groups disgruntled with occupation led guerilla warfare against the Roman occupiers.

King Agrippa II, the hereditary ruler, had been granted power by Rome to appoint the head priest of the Jerusalem temple, which was accordingly a political as much as a religious post. Agrippa's sister, Drusilla, was married to Aziz, king of Emesa. It was a marriage of political convenience. When Antoninus Felix, a former slave, was appointed procurator (governor) of Judaea, Drusilla left Aziz for Felix, whom she soon married. Agrippa had another sister, Bernice, omitted from this story, who he lived with in closer proximity than Jewish custom approved, but which was not out of place in Egypt, where the Pharaoh often married his sister. This perhaps reflected the fact that Agrippa and his sisters spent more time in cosmopolitan Egypt than in Judaea. Their neglect of Judaea, added to their pro-Roman sympathies, meant the Jewish populace had little affection for them.

The marching of a Roman imperial standard into the precincts of the Jerusalem temple, which provides this narrative's climax, occurred in March, 4 BCE. I have shifted it to almost fifty years later because the incident encapsulates the volatility of the populace and the times.

I have drawn on multiple sources. The writings of the Jewish historian, Josephus, provide the imperial standard incident, along with many other details. The representation of the Jerusalem Christians, from whom the Ebionites possibly descended, comes from the New Testament. James the Just, designated 'the brother of the Lord'—an ambiguous title that some have interpreted to mean he was Jesus' actual brother—became head of the Jerusalem community during the thirties or forties. If James was indeed Jesus' brother, then this followed rabbinic custom of having a family member take a dead teacher's place.

The apostle Simon Peter is a fascinating character. Revered today as St Peter, the first Bishop of Rome, when questioned after Jesus' arrest he denied he knew Jesus. He is also a central figure in an most unsavoury incident involving the deaths of the new converts, Anan and Saphirra (see *Acts* 5). My reading is that Peter was more concerned with temporal status and power than with the spiritual virtues advocated by his master.

The final issue I draw attention to here is the place of women in early Christianity. In *Matthew* and *Mark* women are prominent among Jesus' followers, with Mary Magdalene and several other women being the first to witness the risen Christ. However, the Church Fathers refused to include women in their hierarchy. In contrast, many Gnostics gave women equal voice and status in their congregations, as they viewed the female and male principles as having equal and complementary spiritual status. Accordingly, Helen plays a significant role in the version of Simon Magus's story presented here.

Background notes expand on the historical, mythological and philosophic contexts, and underscore my purpose in writing this work: to share scholars' re-evaluations of Christian origins, to emphasise those origins' political, social and metaphysical complexities, and to draw attention to the diverse groups and doctrines that existed in the early centuries, before they were expunged from the official story. Finally, I wish to draw readers' attention to a significant Western spiritual pioneer.

The Gnosis of
Simon Magus

Characters

Simon Magus and his companions
Simon Magus
Helena, also called Miryam
Thomas
Zacharia
Aaron
Joel
Adina
Dositheus

Jerusalem Nazoraeans
Shimon Kepa, apostle
Yacob, leader of Nazoraeans
Zebah
Anan
Sapphira
Nazoraeans

Judaean politicians and religious leaders
Agrippa, King of Judaea
Druscilla, his sister
Ananias, head priest
Hebron, member of Sanhedrin
Mordecai
Jonathan, former head priest

Roman authorities
Antonius Felix, procurator
Lysias, tribune
Marcus
Centurion
Roman soldiers

Others
Endor, a sorceress
Messenger
Girl
Citizens of Jerusalem

Setting Judaea, 52 CE

Jesus said, 'If they ask you, 'Where do you come from?',
answer, 'We come from the self-standing light, which
projects into all images'. If they ask, 'Who are you?', say,
'We are its children, we are the Living Father's chosen.' If
they ask, 'What is the sign of your Father in you?', answer,
'It is movement and repose.'"

— *The Gospel According to Thomas*

Enter Shimon Kepa.

KEPA In the days of King Herod Antipas,
       when Pontius Pilate was procurator here,
       a man named Yeshu left his home in Galilee
       and combed Judaea for revelation.
       He ended on the river Jordan's banks,
       in the presence of naked Yohannes,
       called baptiser by those who revered him.
       Like the desert prophets he emulated,
       Yohannes taught the limitation of
       fleshly existence and the primacy
       of the spiritual realm. He accepted
       Yeshu as one among thirty disciples
       to whom he passed his spiritual knowledge.
       Soon after Yohannes, without arrest
       or trial, was unlawfully murdered
       by Herod's command, but not before the wisdom
       which, for many years, had burned in him,
       was similarly ignited in Yeshu.
       Yohannes' death sent Yeshu back to Galilee
       where, for a people long separated
       from the sources of their own religion,
       he re-opened the shut gates to heaven.
       Three years only he taught, to crowds the length
       of Judaea, then was crucified in turn.
       Today his followers revere his memory

and preach wisdom in his name.
I, Shimon Kepa, Yeshu's first chosen
and chief apostle, guide them, and ensure
Yeshu's saving word is maintained.

Exit Shimon Kepa.

♋ ♋ ♋

The sound of a bird crying, flapping. Enter Simon and Thomas.

SIMON   No further. The flame burns strongest here.
Purify the earth.

Thomas walks around Simon, scattering lighted brands in a circle. Simon signals him to kneel inside it. Simon, also inside the circle, raises his arms.

SIMON   Immortal Fire, kindle in our souls the good,
whether we ask it of you or not;
but command to leave us everything evil,
though ignorantly we beg it of you.
Amen, Amen, Amen-Ra.

Again the sound of a bird crying, flapping.

ENDOR   (*Off*) Simon Magus!
THOMAS   Is it her?
SIMON   The brands.
THOMAS   My hands won't obey me.
SIMON   No matter now. She has come.

Endor remains an off-stage voice.

ENDOR   Simon! Share with me that captive soul
and I'll leave you to conjure in peace.
SIMON   Your power's eclipsed here, Endor.
ENDOR   Fool! My power's everywhere.

Endor shouts. Thunder. A wind starts to howl.

ENDOR   Fasting again, Magus? Your strength's cowered.

SIMON   I have no strength—

ENDOR   Liar!

SIMON   —but that which the Fire manifests through me.

ENDOR   The truth dies on your lips. I know you, Magus.
Your hand reaches far higher than you say.
What point these petty disciplines, this futile fast,
when from Antioch to Idumaea
ten thousand tongues already whisper your name?
Surely hunger gnaws you? Why not work your will,
transform these dry stones into loaves, and eat?
Your pretty boy faints from hunger.

SIMON   Miracles are no sustenance, Endor.
Go your way. I have no quarrel with you.

ENDOR   Mistake, Magus. Trespass into my region
and you conjure a quarrel to the death.

SIMON   By which power?

ENDOR   By the power which is mine!

Thunder. The wind rises. Bird cries, off. Five birds dive down at Simon and Thomas. Simon raises his arms. Light from above illuminates the stage. Simon rises into the air. The birds leave, the wind dies. The light strengthens until it floods the stage with light.

SIMON   Fire and earth are alien elements:
their spheres of influence may commingle,
yet their intents are wholly opposite.
Leave us, witch.
You cannot touch me or mine, though we stand
in the very sanctum of your region.
You threaten only yourself by staying.

ENDOR   Laugh while you may, Simon Magus.
You soon shall feel my power's extension.

Endor shouts. Thunder cracks. Dies. Simon descends.

SIMON   Immortal Fire, deliver us to the good,
but save us from evil. By your will. Amen.

The light fades. Thomas stands, scatters the brands.

SIMON   We have achieved what the powers commanded.
Go back now to Jerusalem's safety
and inform the brothers they should wait.
I must remain in the wilderness here
one night more.

THOMAS   Shalom, master.

SIMON   Shalom, Thomas.

Exit Thomas.

SIMON   You reigning powers, have mercy on us all.

Exit Simon Magus.

♋   ♋   ♋

Shouting, off. Enter Joel and Adina.

JOEL   Magus! For your holy wisdom we suffer.

ADINA   By your name's power may we be saved!

A stone thrown from off-stage strikes Joel and he falls. Enter shouting crowd, throwing stones. Enter Thomas, separately.

CROWD   They follow the magician!—Kill them!—They
want to destroy us!—Kill them now!

Jogging feet, off. A light from above shines onto Joel and Adina. One from the crowd approaches Joel, spits on him, kicks him, picks him up.

THOMAS   Brothers, leave these! You injure yourselves if not.

CITIZEN 1   Leprosy!

Citizen 1 drops Joel. The crowd backs off. The light from above fades. Thomas kneels, takes herbs from out of his bag, applies them to both Joel and Adina.

CROWD   What's he doing?—It's sorcery!—That's because
he follows Simon Magus, too.—Where is the
magician?—He's with the Zealots in Idumaea.—
No!—He was seen there. What else would he do
in the desert?—Kill them now!

The crowd stones Joel, Adina and Thomas. Thomas falls. Enter centurion and soldiers.

CENTURION   Uncurl your claws or our swords shall prune them!
Who disturbs the peace here? On what account?
You! Drop those stones and drag your carcass here.
Soldier!

The soldier drags Citizen 1 to the centurion. Enter Zacharia and Aaron.

CENTURION   By which authority do you stone these men?
You have a tongue. Use it while it yet remains
in your head: I'll feed it to the dogs else.

Citizen 1 spits on the centurion, who knocks him down.

CENTURION   Bring me the head priest, Ananias.

Exit soldier. Another soldier speaks to the centurion.

CENTURION   Leprosy? Who has leprosy?

The crowd indicates Joel. The centurion signals and a soldier examines Joel, shakes his head. The centurion examines Joel himself.

CENTURION   You rioters, animals—whatever you be—
if you know only one law it should be this:
to attempt anarchy by denying,
or subverting, Roman authority
means testing the point of the Roman lance.
And where the Imperial standard has taken root
no local revolt has ever dislodged,
from Gaul to the Rhine, Egypt to Cappodocia.
The Legion arm ensures it.

VOICE   (*Off*) This the plague is with which Yahweh shall strike: all who have fought Jerusalem, their flesh will moulder where they stand, their eyes rot in their sockets, tongues corrupt in their mouths.

The centurion signals to three soldiers, who exit. Citizen 1 is attempting to stand. The centurion kicks him down.

CENTURION   Learn this also: Rome shall not be mocked!

VOICE   (*Off*) None shall remain living; none ever shall claim victory over Yahweh. For He is a scythe, and Rome just chaff to feed Sheol's fires!

The soldiers cross the rear of the stage, exeunt other wing.

CROWD   Freedom! Freedom! Freedom! Freedom!

The centurion signals the soldiers to draw their swords and form ranks. Enter soldier leading Ananias and Hebron. The crowd stops chanting.

ANANIAS   You sent for me?

CENTURION   I requested your presence.

ANANIAS   Don't milk it beyond what it is. What happens here?

CENTURION   Another riot at the temple.

ANANIAS   Substantive grounds are required for any arrest. I assume the same process will adhere under the new procurator?

CENTURION   Antonius Felix arrives tomorrow. You will be informed.

ANANIAS   So why request my presence now?

CENTURION   To discover the circumstances behind the riot.

ANANIAS   I wasn't here.

CENTURION   Soldier, choose six at random to be charged with civil disobedience.

ANANIAS   Wait! You! Were you at the temple? What happened?

CITIZEN 2   The two are followers of the magician, Simon Magus.

CENTURION   So?

HEBRON   What did they do?

CITIZEN 3   Nothing. But they practise magic. It is enough that they were there.

CENTURION   What of the other?

HEBRON   The other?

CITIZEN 4   He was struck when he tried to help.

HEBRON   He wasn't at the Temple?

CITIZEN 4   No.

CENTURION   Who is he?

HEBRON   Do any recognise this man?

CITIZEN 3   He's another of the magician's followers.

CITIZEN 4   His daemon made us see leprosy where there was none.

CENTURION   How many saw this leprosy?

CITIZEN 4   Only him.

CENTURION   Fools! None under Roman rule dies merely for being what he is. Release him. Release them all. Ananias, disperse the crowd.

HEBRON   Their complaint has point. The magician's powers are notorious.

CENTURION   Perhaps. But that is for procurator Antonius Felix to decide when he arrives from Caesarea. I am tasked with maintaining the peace until he does. You may submit complaints at the proper time. And you, Ananias, will subdue your people. The Sanhedrin is bonded to that end. Now disperse. I have authority to impose curfew if required. Go!

Exeunt all but Joel, Adina, Thomas, Zacharia and Aaron.

ZACHARIA   Thomas.

THOMAS   Shalom, brothers.

AARON   You bleed.

THOMAS   More their blood than mine.

ZACHARIA   Where were your thoughts? You knew they
would stone you too.

THOMAS   I was required.

ZACHARIA   To kill yourself?

THOMAS   I saw an angel hovering over them. You didn't
see it?

ZACHARIA   And I didn't feel the air beaten by its wings.

THOMAS   Angels don't have wings.

ZACHARIA   Fasting has made you delirious. Where's the
Magus?

THOMAS   He arrives tomorrow.

ZACHARIA   Come, before the crowd returns to finish what
Rome only allowed them to begin.

Exeunt.

♋   ♋   ♋

Singing, off. Enter Helena and Dositheus.

HELENA   Master Dositheus, do not think me
ungrateful for the love I have received
from you and those here who practise your way.
Each day I wake amazed to find myself
at home among such rituals as these,
since what I am is so utterly opposed
to all you have set yourselves to achieve.
But that is what I do not understand:
why should you welcome me so tenderly
when I am what you so patently are not?

DOSITHEUS   Answer me a question first: what are you
that you should cause us this supposed offence?

HELENA   You don't know? I'm appalled. I can't say it.
          Surely, when the Magus delivered me here,
          he informed you of my occupation.
DOSITHEUS Simon said he found you in Tyre's brothels,
          from which he purchased you your freedom.
HELENA   So you do know.
DOSITHEUS But that is not my question's answer.
          Prostitution is only what you did;
          I asked you what you are.
HELENA   I'm confused. We know what we are by what we do.
DOSITHEUS You're wrong. Those who perceive the skin only
          may speak so, for they live by externals.
          But we are more than merely what we do.
HELENA   I am now lost completely.
DOSITHEUS You think because you lived in sin, we here
          who practise austerity should condemn you?
HELENA   Jerusalem's holy would stone me if they could.
DOSITHEUS Jerusalem's holy judge by acts alone:
          they assume one who lives in sin is sinful,
          and hence should be condemned. But they are
              blind.
          We are, in our deepest nature, of God.
          If ever we sin, we do so only
          because we forget what, in truth, we are.
          Further, as God is perfect and pure,
          so God in us cannot be stained with sin,
          which means a sinful act may be reproved,
          but God's presence within forbids condemnation.
          It would be blasphemy to attempt so.
          Hence neither do we condemn you.
HELENA   Thank you, master.
          Yet that does not explain your welcome's warmth,
          nor why I was permitted here at all.

	This is no rest-house; I see no other guests.
	So why am I accepted where none else is?
DOSITHEUS	For that you must question Simon Magus.
HELENA	When will I have the opportunity?
DOSITHEUS	Shortly.
HELENA	He is here?
DOSITHEUS	Since noon. He leads the prayers.
HELENA	Gone forty days, he returns without comment?
	Why was I not informed?

The singing ends. Enter Simon Magus.

DOSITHEUS	Consider yourself, sister. You're a guest here;
	you do not own the keys to the house.
HELENA	And that's another point. All here say 'sister'.
	My name is Helena. Why isn't it used?
SIMON	Permit me to answer that.
HELENA	Magus!
DOSITHEUS	Shalom, brother.
SIMON	Shalom, Dositheus.
	Sister, rise. Only God deserves our worship.
	I trust you have had a peaceful visit?
HELENA	I have. Please complete what you were saying.
SIMON	Sister, none here call you Helena
	because Helena was never your name.
HELENA	They happily called me that in Tyre.
SIMON	Perhaps. But you have died to that life now.
	Unless you desire its return?
HELENA	Of course not.
SIMON	Did you not come here by choice?
HELENA	Once my freedom was bought, I had no life left
	to pursue, but the journey you offered.
	I gladly came.
DOSITHEUS	Your presence pleases us also.

SIMON   Dositheus and I were pupils once,
            long ago, of Yohannes, a hard man
            who lived many years in the wilderness,
            fasting and praying that he might find God.
            Thirty disciples shared that search with him
            until his murder by Herod Antipas,
            when each chose to go his separate way.
            Some died; some gave up; some found another
                path.
            I sought Alexandria's wisdom, to learn
            Egyptian philosophy and magic;
            Dositheus remained, sustaining our
            desert community with love and knowledge.
            My purpose in suggesting you stay here
            was singular: to help you remember.
            You had a life before the brothels of Tyre,
            and in that life you owned another name.
            My aim is that you should rediscover it.
HELENA   You know what it is?
SIMON   I do.
HELENA   And master Dositheus?
DOSITHEUS   Yes.
HELENA   Why not tell me?
DOSITHEUS   Because it would mean nothing to you.
SIMON   You must remember the life behind the name.
HELENA   Before Tyre I remember nothing. Did I live here?
SIMON   You visited. But this was not your home.
HELENA   My hands are trembling. What happened to me
            that my conscious mind should become a blank?
            Something in me knows, doesn't it?
SIMON   The peace here, as we hoped, has helped still
            the sensual impediments Tyre stirred,
            while austerities have purified your heart.

Our next step is to visit Jerusalem
where perhaps the shock of recognition
will return to mind the past you have lost.
We leave tomorrow, at dawn.

DOSITHEUS   Brother, I'll furnish provisions and a guide.
Tell me what else you need, and it is yours.
But now I hope you'll eat with us one last time.

SIMON   With pleasure. Sister.

Exeunt.

♋   ♋   ♋

Enter Aaron, Zacharia and Thomas.

ZACHARIA   Why meet here? A bare room would have served
as well to voice your news.

AARON   You would not then have seen for yourselves.

ZACHARIA   Seen what?

AARON   Down there.

ZACHARIA   The Magus' house?

AARON   Examine the neighbouring roof.

ZACHARIA   Who's that man?

AARON   He, or another, have watched these five days past.

ZACHARIA   Spies. Roman?

AARON   The Sanhedrin's.
They fear the crowds Simon lately has drawn,
swayed by his powers, will quit the Temple
and forgo the Law's prescribed rituals,
diminishing thus their influence—

ZACHARIA   And their revenue, which is more the point.
What god rules this world that he should approve
idiots as his earthly representatives?

AARON   Idiots perhaps, but dangerous too.
Should we not somehow forewarn the Magus?

ZACHARIA	When is his planned return? You saw him last.
THOMAS	He said he required one further night only.
AARON	Rumours fill Jerusalem that Simon,
	seen no doubt in Idumaea with you,
	has joined a bandit group of Zealots.
ZACHARIA	Which rumour the Romans also have heard?
AARON	Their spies skulk in every market.
ZACHARIA	Thomas, what public denial should we make?
THOMAS	You know the master's thoughts on Zealots.
ZACHARIA	Wake up, man! Angels so dazzle his eyes
	he can't see the devils threatening us.
AARON	Thomas spoke the truth.
ZACHARIA	But don't you see our situation here?
	It's not truth, but Roman perception of truth
	that we must make the focus of our study.
	How we stand in our own eyes is nothing;
	but how we appear to stand in Roman,
	in the Sanhedrin's eyes—that is all.
	They decide our life and death. None else.
	We must consider them, whatever we do.

Enter Joel and Adina.

THOMAS	Shalom, brothers.
AARON	Joel. Adina.
JOEL	Shalom.
ZACHARIA	Where are the others?
ADINA	They've gone.
ZACHARIA	Where? To Idumaea?
JOEL	No, journeying.
ADINA	Permanently.
ZACHARIA	Deserted? Shama, perhaps. But Malachi, Heman,
	Asaph, the others?
ADINA	All gone.

ZACHARIA   Why?

JOEL   Surely Aaron told you?

ADINA   They feared for their lives.

ZACHARIA   Cowards! I'd kill them myself if they showed. No; I'm pleased. Better abandon us now, than when their aid is necessitous later. We five are enough. Simon's safe with us.

ADINA   There's a new rumour current.

ZACHARIA   About the Zealots? We heard.

JOEL   No, another.

ADINA   Travellers from Tyre told us.

JOEL   The Magus has a prostitute.

ADINA   Her name is Helena. He calls her an angel, and proclaims he raised her from the dead.

JOEL   Something like that.

ADINA   The markets are buzzing.

JOEL   They've been seen in Idumaea, too.

ADINA   For your sakes, I pray he won't bring her here.

ZACHARIA   For our sakes? Why not for yours?

JOEL   Zacharia, our families have been threatened.

ADINA   Please understand.

JOEL   They've sent men to my brother's house.

ADINA   And mine.

ZACHARIA   Who have?

JOEL   The Sanhedrin.

ADINA   If only our own lives were at issue we would not now be craving indulgence.

JOEL   Our families are innocent.

ADINA   We can't let them suffer for our acts.

JOEL   Stay away!

AARON   Zacharia, daggers solve nothing.

JOEL   We're not deserting.

ADINA   Merely retreating.

ZACHARIA Scum!

JOEL We'll be back.

ADINA When it's safer.

JOEL For our families.

ADINA We're still your brothers in truth.

ZACHARIA Liars! Get out of my sight! Let me go.

Exeunt Joel and Adina.

ZACHARIA Why must I be the only one who thinks? United we can act; separate, we're nothing.

THOMAS Surely they are safer away from us.

ZACHARIA Whose side are you on?

THOMAS Conscience takes no sides, but serves the good.

ZACHARIA Thomas, you're too naive for your own good. Let's hope we're able to warn the Magus. For today we'll remain out of public eye.

Exeunt.

♋   ♋   ♋

Enter Antonius Felix, Marcus and soldiers, one of whom carries an Imperial Standard.

FELIX So this is the land I am to rule. Tell me, Marcus, are these people truly as bereft of reason as their countryside is of cultivated land?

MARCUS Do not underestimate the their cunning, Antonius. Or their courage. We hold the cities and their environs. But a detachment of less than twenty cannot safely patrol the mountains, or even the unfortified countryside. The Zealots have strong peasant support.

FELIX Roman intelligence says they are too disjointed to provide long-lasting opposition. I feel my time as

procurator here will prove Judaea's final taming.
What is that city below?

MARCUS   Ain Karim, excellency.

FELIX   Its distance from Jerusalem?

MARCUS   A half day's march.

FELIX   Set up camp within its walls. The men need rest
before we march tomorrow into Jerusalem and
show these rebels who is their true master. And
Marcus.

MARCUS   Yes, my lord?

FELIX   Find a necromancer for tonight's entertainment.
I would like to enjoy my time here in at least a
semblance of Roman fashion.

Exeunt.

᪥   ᪥   ᪥

*Thunder. Enter Lysias, accompanied by soldiers who march between
them three citizens. Each prisoner carries a crossbar. A silent crowd of
Jerusalem's citizens enters, watches. The soldiers nail the citizens' wrists
to the crossbars. The prisoners scream.*

WOMAN   My son!

*The soldiers nail the prisoners' heels to the uprights. The woman shrieks,
throws herself onto the soldiers. They throw her back. The crowd re-
sponds by picking up stones and presenting staffs. Enter Ananias.*

ANANIAS   Enough! These men are dead. You can do no more.

*The crowd throws down its stones, lowers its staffs. The soldiers hoist
the three crosses, with men attached, into position.*

ANANIAS   They should fitly applaud Felix's entry.

LYSIAS   Each wears rebellion's stain.

ANANIAS   Do not misunderstand me, Lysias.
I appreciate your concern. Four months

in dungeons have made them pale: a day's
    sunning
is sure to relieve their flagging spirits.
Tell me, Lysias, you hear all Roman news.
Is what rumour whispers of Caesar true?

LYSIAS   There are always rumours.

ANANIAS   This says disease has so rotted Caesar's brain
that reason is banished from the Empire.

LYSIAS   Softly, Ananias; I have limits.

ANANIAS   True. But we here breath the Empire's limits,
while great Nero thinks of us so little
he sends a former slave to stride Judaea
like a petty self-preening colossus.

LYSIAS   Among Rome's wise are many former slaves.
As procurator, Antonius Felix,
Caesar's full weight behind him, may exercise
his power to the law's considered compass.

ANANIAS   Does marching standards into Jerusalem
fall inside or outside the law's compass?

LYSIAS   Why?

ANANIAS   His cohort carries standards to the fore.

LYSIAS   How do you know?

ANANIAS   They've been seen.

LYSIAS   Where?

ANANIAS   Joppa.

LYSIAS   That's three days' march away.
He will take them down between there and here.

ANANIAS   They've batted the air from Caesarea.
And they stand now in Ain Karim.

LYSIAS   He will take them down, I say.

ANANIAS   How can you say? You know nothing of what
Felix will do: you're his toy as much as we.
Support me as head priest in the Temple

and I'll use my power to smooth civil unrest
and placate the chafings of the Sanhedrin.
But let Felix thrust his standards into
Jerusalem, and I shall not hinder
what slaughter will immediately follow.
More, I myself shall urge the city to it;
I'll shriek till the ramparts be bathed in blood.
We walk backwards: not since Pontius Pilate
smeared Judaea with his vile blasphemies
have we been as ignorantly blighted.
You had best inform this strutting Felix
no pagan image must foul the Temple's precincts.
Jerusalem shall burn to the ground first.

Exit Ananias.

LYSIAS   Bring me Jonathan. And remove this rabble.
            Their stink is almost more than I can stand.

Exit soldier. The centurion signals other soldiers, who push back the crowd. Enter Jonathan.

LYSIAS   Welcome Jonathan. Thank you for attending.
JONATHAN   It's my pleasure to speak to Rome.
LYSIAS   I understand that in your term as head priest
            here, you recommended the election in Rome of
            Antonius Felix to the position of procurator?
JONATHAN   I did.
LYSIAS   In matters of policy, then, he sits in your pocket?
JONATHAN   He owes me certain considerations. No less; no
            more.
LYSIAS   Did you know he would march standards into
            Jerusalem?
JONATHAN   Surely not. The city will revolt.
LYSIAS   Perhaps your influence could persuade him of
            his folly.

JONATHAN	This is the Sanhedrin's business. And yours. None of mine.
LYSIAS	If you help me, I'll assist you.
JONATHAN	In what do I require assistance?
LYSIAS	I dislike Ananias. He's outgrown his authority. You were head priest once. Would you enjoy filling that position again?
JONATHAN	King Agrippa selects the head priest.
LYSIAS	He is pliable. You have supporters in the Sanhedrin?
JONATHAN	Ananias has enemies.
LYSIAS	I think we have sufficient common cause to continue this discussion in greater depth. (To centurion) Dismiss the guards. These won't leap to freedom. (To Jonathan) After you.

Exeunt.

♋   ♋   ♋

Enter King Agrippa, followed by servants and messenger.

AGRIPPA	Who is this Antonius Felix? Is he mad? Does he not know Jerusalem will revolt? Druscilla! Bring her here. Where's my powder? This desert air torments my complexion. Well? You have no other nightmares to tell?
MESSENGER	Majesty, I speak only my duty.
AGRIPPA	Then speak it. I'm ready. No, this side first.
MESSENGER	The High Priest, Ananias, bid me say -
AGRIPPA	Must I do it all myself? Give it me. The mirror. Continue.
MESSENGER	Antonius Felix is camped tonight in Ain Karim, half a day from Jerusalem. He seems determined to carry standards bearing Nero's face onto sanctified ground.

	You know the catastrophe this will fire.
	Ananias begs your intervention.
AGRIPPA	I shall indeed intervene. The arrogance!
	When he is no more than Ceasar's puppet.
	I am Judaea's sole ruler and king;
	he'll do nothing without my permission!
	Enough. Enough, I say. Would you be whipped?

Enter Druscilla.

AGRIPPA	Druscilla, my darling sister. How do you feel?
DRUSCILLA	None the better for this wilderness trek.
	Being king of Judaea is one thing,
	but actually to visit—this is hell.
	Can't you rule from Egypt like everyone else?
AGRIPPA	You are an angel for what you endure.
	I have good news. The new procurator,
	Antonius Felix, has sent his respects
	and begs our presence at his banquet tonight.
DRUSCILLA	Where is he?
AGRIPPA	Ain Karim.
DRUSCILLA	That's hours away.
AGRIPPA	It appears I am a pretext only:
	you are the true object of his feasting.
DRUSCILLA	I am?
AGRIPPA	So his messenger here informed me.
DRUSCILLA	Is this true?
AGRIPPA;	Tell her.
MESSENGER	My lady, it is.
DRUSCILLA	Give me fifteen minutes to prepare.

Exit Druscilla.

AGRIPPA	Send word to this Antonius Felix
	my sister and I shall feast with him at dusk.
	Say whatever you will; just arrange it.

But make him proper obeisance: despite
this fault, his voice in Judaea is Caesar's.

Exit servant.

AGRIPPA You shall carry word to Ananias
we enter Jerusalem with Felix.
For the rest, I'll send letters later. Go.

Exit messenger.

AGRIPPA Saddle the Arabian stallions.
Well? Did you not hear my sister's command?
In fifteen minutes we depart.

Exeunt.

♋   ♋   ♋

Enter Simon Magus and Helena.

SIMON Sister, there's little time before our presence
on Jerusalem's outskirts is discovered,
and there is much we have not discussed.

HELENA Magus, let me first express my gratitude.
These few short months since you bought my
    freedom
I have received more thoughtfulness from you
than I could ever have believed my due.
Truly, I am not convinced I deserve it,
so desperately lived were my former days.
When I wake each morning, I fear to open
my eyes in case this adventure
proves only to be a wonderful dream.
Yet look: my cheeks truly are wet.

SIMON Sister, relax.
The life you lived has died to you forever;
now another awaits your return.

HELENA So you say. But I remember nothing.
        Tell me, why did you purchase my freedom?
        You've never responded when I asked.
SIMON   Not from my own volition. I was told.
HELENA By whom?
SIMON   By those who occupy a secret place
        wherein your real name is recorded.
HELENA And that place is here, in Jerusalem?
SIMON   It is both nearer, and more distant, than that.
HELENA I don't understand.
SIMON   Be silent, and you shall.

Simon kneel and Helena kneel. They face one another, eyes closed. Light from above gradually fills the stage, reaching a blinding level. Helena rises into the air. Simon claps. Helena descends. The light recedes.

SIMON   Do you understand now?
HELENA I saw my name. Or rather, I saw two,
        one superimposed over the other.
        The exterior name was Miryam;
        the interior name was Sophia.
SIMON   Sophia is your spiritual title;
        Miryam your name while living on this earth.
        You don't seem pleased.
VOICES (*Off*) Over there.—I saw him only a few minutes
        ago, passing the ridge.—He can't be far away.
MIRYAM Dositheus was right. Knowing my name
        has not brought back to memory the life
        I lived before I arrived in Tyre.
SIMON   The point is, you discovered it yourself.

Enter several Citizens.

CITIZENS Magus, where have you been?—We've waited
          weeks for your return.—My family is starving.—

Magus, you must help me.—Me first, my need is
greater.—Please! Save us from death!

SIMON   What foolishness is this? Are you human?
Then do not behave like dogs. Stand and speak.

CITIZEN 5   Please, Magus. See my arms. Disease has eaten
their strength. I can no longer work, and my family
starves. You're my last hope. You must cure me.

CITIZEN 6   I am losing my sight. Each passing week reduces
my vision. Only your magic can make me see.

Enter Zacharia, Thomas and Aaron.

CITIZEN 7   Magus, last week my father died. My cousins
now have claimed his goods, which rightfully
belong to me. I beg you use your powers to win
them back.

ZACHARIA   Magus, who are these swine which bother you?
Say the word and I'll drive them away.

SIMON   Stay where you are. And you three hear my voice.
You say you are an innocent victim,
that justice is abused by your cousins' greed.
Yet your avarice plainly equals theirs.
Why should I take sides in such a contest?
Fight among yourselves; I refuse your hate.
As for you two liars, speak not as if God
or I could give you health, which comes only
to those who truly desire and deserve it;
for you take to wine as fish to water
and destroy what health has been given you.
Observe your state: you both can walk and smile;
neither leprosy eats your limbs, nor do
devils inhabit your thoughts. What evil
is there in that? Rather, count your blessings,
and abstain from wine; clouding the soul,

[41]

it makes the world seem darker than it is.
And try at least to learn sincerity,
not to remain nothings your entire lives.
Who else here desires my counsel?

CITIZEN 8 Magus, forgive me. But I am a desperate man.

SIMON Speak.

CITIZEN 8 My daughter, Magus. She—she—

SIMON No-one watches, my son. You're safe from prying eyes.

CITIZEN 8 I would be whipped if any at the Temple learned I sought your wisdom.

SIMON None shall, unless you tell them. What troubles your daughter?

CITIZEN 8 Yesterday she ate diseased dates. Last night she vomited blood. Now she's dying. Here. I have money. I have—take this robe. I would give you anything. If only my daughter doesn't—

SIMON How long since you saw your daughter?

CITIZEN 8 Five hours. I heard you were seen and waited out here all that time.

SIMON The fever has broken. She will outlive you.

CITIZEN 8 Thank you, Magus. Thank you.

SIMON I did nothing. She was already safe. Give him your robe, the remainder your coins. Now depart.

Exeunt Citizens.

ZACHARIA Magus, why refuse the money? We are not rich, and could have used it as usefully as they.

SIMON Powers received gratis must be exercised
gratis: they turn on the vehicle else,
destroying what would otherwise produce.

ZACHARIA And what will those idiots produce but
more misery for themselves and others?

SIMON   We each act according to our nature;
remember that in the trials to come.
Thomas, our sister Miryam requires
protection while she visits Jerusalem.
I trust she may anticipate that from you?

THOMAS   With pleasure.

SIMON   Yes, Aaron. What of the others?

AARON   Departed.

ZACHARIA   With their tails between their legs.

SIMON   They waited much longer than they might.
Let's leave ourselves before others return
and seek recompense for their chosen failings.
What else you need to know I'll tell you shortly.

Exeunt.

♋   ♋   ♋

Enter Kepa, Yacob, Zebah, Anan, Sapphira, and other Nazoraeans.

KEPA   Brothers, sisters: what great pleasure this brings.
Surely the Spirit breathes through us all that
we again should be safely gathered thus.
You look dishevelled. Where have you come
from?

ZEBAH   The place of crucifixions.

ANAN   Sapphira's cousin, master. He is—

KEPA   Do you intend to follow Yeshu's teaching?

ANAN   You know we do.

KEPA   The path he taught is not an easy path.
A single rider cannot mount two horses;
nor can one servant obey two masters.
Just so must we embrace unity,
if purpose suit refusing our own flesh and blood,
becoming strangers and nomads upon the earth,

that we may justly follow Yeshu's commands
and stand one day among the elect.

SAPPHIRA I'm to blame. I asked my husband, Anan,
to pray with me for those shortly to die.
We meant no harm.

KEPA Few mean harm, but they do it just the same.
How was you cousin captured?

SAPPHIRA He was betrayed.

KEPA Tell us here by whom.

ANAN By his brother.

KEPA And still you doubt my call to unity?

YACOB None here doubts the undeniable, Kepa.
But let us not forget our reason today
for meeting thus is to welcome Anan
and Sapphira into our community.
Obedient to our strictures, they have sold
their house and all their earthly possessions,
and passed to me the full sum resulting
to alleviate the want among us.
I myself welcome them most lovingly;
I know each here feels the same.

KEPA We do, brother.
But neither do we forget that to renounce
the world is but the first step to election.
There yet remains surrender to Yahweh's will,
and to the Word by which that will is revealed.
Inspired by Yahweh, Moses promised
a great prophet would rise from among us,
saying whoever ignored that prophet
would be cut off from Yahweh's revelation.
That prophet has lived and died in the world.
His name is Yeshu, the son of Yoseph,
descended of our great King David.

Yet while our greatest prophesied long ago
one of the house of David would succeed
to his throne, Yeshu, our Lord God's chosen,
came and went unnoticed by all but a few.
This is the truth: Yahweh sent Word to Judaea,
the good news of peace that Yeshu pronounced,
but foolish Judaea refused to listen.
I was there; I witnessed it; I know.
Thousands in Galilee, and Jerusalem too,
sought Yeshu's love, wisdom, and healing touch;
yet though they looked, they did not truly see
what power worked miracles amongst them.
Jealousy, not worship, was Yeshu's reward.
Thus plots arose, and those very people
Yeshu was sent to save turned against him,
threw him to Rome and, like any common
criminal, he was crucified on a tree.
Yet Yahweh never abandons his own.
Three days later Yeshu rose from the dead
and was seen, not by the whole people, but
by certain witnesses the Lord's will chose.
We are those witnesses; the faithful to whom
Yeshu appeared and commanded that we
preach the truth to ignorant Judaea.
This we have done to our power's capacity.
Yet just as the faithful stand preferred to
the unfaithful, so some have witnessed more
than their brothers. As tradition dictates
Yacob, Yeshu's brother, was elected
head of our nascent community here,
for which he enjoys our love and respect.
But he was not there in the beginning.
I was. Three years I followed our master,

breaking his bread, sharing his cup, learning
the wisdom Yahweh empowered him to preach.
And so astute was I, so percipient
of his aims, that before his death Yeshu
named me Kepa, the rock, upon whose back
the burden of his holy teaching rests.
Other apostles arrived, fell, were replaced;
Yacob was chosen to administer
to our physical wants; but I remain,
first called, loyal still, chief witness, guide and
spiritual interpreter of the Word
Yahweh pronounced through our master Yeshu,
which Word we are commanded to maintain
until, as prophesied, Yeshu returns,
takes up his Messiah's crown, purifies
the Jerusalem Temple, and judges
the living and the dead, rewarding each
according to his or her adherence
to the ancient faith of our forefathers.
Anan, Sapphira, do not underweigh
the commitment you both are here to make.
We are the faithful, the chosen elect;
we justify Yeshu's crucifixion.
The hope for a new Jerusalem rests in us.

YACOB Zebah, is all prepared?

ZEBAH It is.

YACOB Anan, Sapphira, after all you have heard from Shimon Kepa's mouth, you still desire to join our Jerusalem community?

ANAN We do.

YACOB Let us walk within, then, and hear your vows.

Exeunt.

♋ ♋ ♋

Enter Antonius Felix and Jonathan, accompanied by servants.

FELIX   Three days in Judaea, and I have seen
   more crucifixions than my entire outward
   journey from Corinth to Caesarea.

JONATHAN   It's under Roman law they're crucified.

FELIX   Does Rome make them pillage, riot, revolt?
   I see my rule as procurator here
   needs strength's immediate application.
   Where's the necromancer I ordered brought in?

ATTENDANT   On her way, my lord.

FELIX   You made quick time from Jerusalem.

JONATHAN   I was chased.

FELIX   By Zealots?

JONATHAN   By my conscience.
   Felix, I supported your election
   in Rome because I thought your judgement fair.
   Yet by this one act you will undo
   a generation's stumbling steps to peace.
   Surely you realise how many will die
   if you march standards into Jerusalem?

FELIX   How so? I seek merely to remind this
   forgetful land that great Caesar in Rome
   is its remote, but vigilant, ruler.

JONATHAN   Granted. But Rome has ever allowed us
   the privilege of worshipping but one god,
   Yahweh Sabaoth, whose holy presence
   has filled our Temple since first time began.
   Many before Rome conquered our lands;
   none yet have defiled the Temple by setting
   within its precincts a pagan image.
   Yet this sanctuary with standards you would
   now invade. Jerusalem won't take it.
   I warn you, thousands will die in the repelling.

FELIX   Thousands? You exaggerate.
JONATHAN   Our Lord said plainly: Worship no foreign god.
            Your standards broadcast Nero's image.
            We allow that to Rome he may be a god,
            and give him tribute as the defeated must;
            but place your standards on sanctified ground
            and war shall erupt. Yahweh commands it.
FELIX   Until now I was blind to Judaea's plight;
            thank you, Jonathan, for peeling my eyes.
            Yet examine this now from Caesar's view.
            Rome's rule extends from Gaul to Cappodocia.
            The most warlike nations today bow before
            the Imperial Standard and peacefully
            accept their destinies, revel in them even,
            for Rome's glory is equally their own.
            Athens, Macedonia, Sicily,
            Egypt, Lucia—what need I go on.
            Even the five hundred cities of Asia,
            without a garrison, to one governor
            and the consular fasces pay their excise.
            Why should Judaea be the sole exception?
            Few in Rome know, or care, about you Jews.
            We could massacre the whole populace
            and history would not remember you,
            you are of such paltry consequence.
            However, that is not the Roman way.
            We seek peace; hence our first attempt will be
            to exercise peaceful means. But let that fail,
            and violence will be executed.
            I don't apologise for refusing you:
            Rome's weight of aspirations rests on me.
            I shall do what I must.

Enter attendant.

FELIX   Well?

ATTENDANT   The necromancer is on her way. King Agrippa has arrived also, with Druscilla, his sister.

FELIX   Bring them in.

Exit attendant.

FELIX   King Agrippa this morning sent word that he and his sister are left Alexandria to greet me. As Judaea's ruler, his wisdom and authority must be acknowledged.

Enter attendant with Endor.

FELIX   I entertain tonight in full Roman style; yet our feastings will be the richer, Jonathan, for your presence. Do not allow a minor disagreement to sever our long friendship. I expect you there.

JONATHAN   I will attend, your excellency.

Exit Jonathan.

FELIX   Woman, you are here because my servants commended your powers of sorcery. I myself am doubtful. Rome is legendary for its necromancers. Yet if you can perform half what your advocates promise, you should prove diverting entertainment. You read palms, I assume?

ENDOR   I prefer the stars.

FELIX   You do? What of cards and crystals?

ENDOR   For children on wet days, perhaps. For adults I prefer entrails.

FELIX   Of beast or foul?

ENDOR   They are hardly adequate for satisfying Roman proclivities.

FELIX   This is wonderful. Perhaps Judaea is not so barren after all. What's your name?

ENDOR   Endor.

FELIX   Do me adequate service, and you'll receive more than adequate reward.

ENDOR   I am yours.

ATTENDANT   Agrippa, King of Judaea, and Druscilla, his sister.

Enter Agrippa and Druscilla, with entourage.

FELIX   My royal brother in authority, Rome stretches its arms in heartfelt welcome.

AGRIPPA   Antonius Felix, Judaea welcomes you. Allow me to introduce Druscilla.

FELIX   I stand ravished. Roman report scarcely pays homage to the exquisiteness of your beauty.

DRUSCILLA   I am pleased Alexandria is not as far from Rome as silence leads us sometimes to think.

FELIX   If Rome neglects her tributaries, she would appear to suffer the greater loss. I trust in my time here I may redress a fault no-one knowingly would commit. A banquet tonight is prepared. I pray you will adorn it with your presence and set the required redress in motion.

DRUSCILLA   I could not disappoint a prayer which is so sweetly petitioned. We are honoured.

FELIX   Are the baths prepared?

ATTENDANT   They are.

FELIX   Warmed goats' milk will wash the dust from your skin; and there's aged wine to refresh the palate.

DRUSCILLA   I am grateful. You may take my arm.

FELIX   King Agrippa.

AGRIPPA   Go ahead. I'll follow. Old woman.

Exeunt Felix, Druscilla, and attendants.

AGRIPPA   Are you the Endor whose powers ended a drought last year in Gaza?

ENDOR   I am.

AGRIPPA   Does Felix know this?

ENDOR   He does not.

AGRIPPA   What can you do with herbs and plants?

ENDOR   I have my knowledge.

AGRIPPA   Could you mix me a potion?

ENDOR   What kind?

AGRIPPA   A love potion.

ENDOR   To achieve what?

AGRIPPA   Ears surround us. I must to the baths. Come to my servants shortly. They shall inform you of my wants, and obtain for you the necessary ingredients. Judaea appreciates your loyal service.

Exit Agrippa. Endor motions. Thunder. Exit Endor.

♋   ♋   ♋

Enter Ananias and messenger.

ANANIAS   That's all Agrippa said?

MESSENGER   Once he has spoken to Antonius Felix, letters will follow.

ANANIAS   Agrippa's looks are the same?

Enter Hebron.

MESSENGER   They are.

ANANIAS   As well he stays in Egypt as much as he does. Go now, but stand ready. What's this I hear of Simon Magus? Does he really have a whore?

Exit messenger.

HEBRON   Bought her in Tyre. Rumour says he proclaims her an angel.

ANANIAS   Could he play into our hands so easily? There must be some deviousness behind his actions.

HEBRON   We shall soon find out. He arrived in Jerusalem
          several hours ago.

ANANIAS   With the whore? What of the crowds? Last time
          he visited the city buzzed for months.

HEBRON   Word is he raised a girl from the dead while still
          outside the city gates. Naturally, some among
          the more vocal already name him Messiah.

ANANIAS   Even better. The whore will help discredit him.
          But we require more than that, and the Romans
          will happily crucify any messiahs we bring them.
          This should prove a fruitful night.

Exeunt.

♋   ♋   ♋

*Music and dancing heard, off. Enter Agrippa and Endor. Endor gives
Agrippa a jug of wine. They talk briefly. Bones are thrown onto the
stage. Four citizens enter, see the bones, fight over them. A soldier enters,
beats them. Exeunt Agrippa and Endor.*

SOLDIER   These bones are for the procurator's dogs. Get
          your thieving hands away.

*Exeunt citizens. Enter dancers and musicians, followed by Antonius
Felix, Druscilla, Agrippa, Jonathan, Endor, courtiers and soldiers.*

FELIX   Agrippa, your sister's beauty illumes
          our revels past even Roman measure.

AGRIPPA   Brother, refresh yourself.
          This wine, a secret family vintage,
          is sure to redeem your extended breath.

FELIX   There's but the one cup?

AGRIPPA   This wine is drunk by Judaea's kings only.

Agrippa drinks, passes the cup to Felix.

FELIX   I am honoured. To friendship.

AGRIPPA Brother, all at once. Please.
This cup seals our mutual authority.
From this moment on, Judaea's kingly line
stands behind you, Antonius Felix.
Druscilla, welcome our new-fledged brother.
Music!

Druscilla and Felix dance.

FELIX I hope I am not dancing her too hard
I would not want such a flower to wilt.
DRUSCILLA My lord, the flower can speak for herself.
Believe me, such exertions are common here.
We are not a pansied race.
FELIX Madam, I envy your husband his luck
in securing such a prize for his bed.
DRUSCILLA My lord, you remind me of a thing
which your presence has driven from my mind.
FELIX My least intention is to annoy you.
DRUSCILLA Then do not speak of him again.
FELIX My dear lady Druscilla, I shall not;
provided you grant me first a favour.
DRUSCILLA Not so loud; we are not alone.
FELIX I meant only we should dispense with titles,
which are for enemies and inferiors,
not for equals who must rule together.
So call me Antonius, please.
DRUSCILLA I thank you, on both our behalfs, and trust
our intimacy shall grow quickly from this,
a most pleasurable planting.
FELIX I must admit, I saw my time from Rome
in terms of exile; but you have altered my view.
DRUSCILLA You'll be surprised to learn, Antonius,
that while a land of tradesmen and peasants,

yet we are not as agricultural as we seem.
Indeed, jaded Roman appetites find
new life here, and as Antony in Egypt
discovered fresh spring, so I am convinced
that you in Judaea shall sip pleasures
of a sophistication consistent
with a people in fact older than Rome's.

FELIX   My blood races. I fear I've out-danced myself.
Enough!

AGRIPPA   Wine, brother, to cool yourself.

FELIX   Thank you, Agrippa.
Soldier, tell Marcus we are ready.

Exit soldier.

FELIX   Is the sorceress here?

ENDOR   I am, excellency.

FELIX   As climax to our entertainment tonight,
and to issue in our mutual reign,
I have arranged the performance for us
of an ancient Roman ritual,
to find if we have the gods' approval,
or if our rule here must labour in darkness.

Enter Marcus and soldier, with three citizens in chains.

DRUSCILLA   Is not Caesar's approval sufficient?

FELIX   In power's terms. But I lack yet your brother's.

DRUSCILLA   We are not gods.

FELIX   Madam, you have the aspect of a goddess.

DRUSCILLA   I'm sure I speak for Agrippa when I say
both approval, and accommodation,
will not be difficult to obtain.

FELIX   Endor, which of these best suits your purpose?

ENDOR   The dark one.

FELIX   Marcus, see to it.

Exeunt Marcus, soldier, and three chained citizens.

ENDOR   Lower the lights, and set this incense burning.

The courtiers obey. A man screams, off. Endor indicates a square.

ENDOR   To sustain the invocation's power
               each of you must occupy a corner square;
               I myself shall occupy the centre.

Agrippa, Druscilla, Felix and Jonathan take up the indicated positions. Enter a soldier, carrying a covered platter. Enter Simon Magus above, flying. Endor takes the platter, places it in the square's centre, takes off the lid. The platter contains the internal organs of the sacrificed prisoner. Jonathan moves to one side, vomits. Felix grabs a courtier, puts him in place in the square. Endor chants. A bird cries, off. Endor motions. Thunder. Enter five birds, crying, flying across the stage. Endor becomes possessed.

ENDOR   Belial!
               Beware those who doubt your word. Strike them
                  down
               before they would strike at you. Kill them all!
               Beware those who smile, but lie. Cut their tongues!
               Beware those whose acts are—Simon Magus!
               I know you are here. I feel your presence.
               Felix, there is magic ranged against you.
               Beware the magician who—Beware!—Beware!

Exit Simon Magus. The birds depart. The thunder ends.

FELIX   Bravo! See to her comfort. Well, brother,
               was not that a voice inspired by reason?
AGRIPPA   It was.
JONATHAN   Antonius Felix, I object.
               You must not follow this foul hag's ravings.
FELIX   Must not? You dare command me?
JONATHAN   She manipulates you to her own ends.

FELIX   You are jealous because your impotent god,
             Yahweh, lacks the power to inspire.
JONATHAN   Her inspiration is madness, no more.
             Judaea trembles on a precipice
             one insignificant act sends thousands
             marauding the streets, seeking new blood to spill.
             Such violence is not ended through violence,
             but by concession and mutual respect.
             Her words are provocative of genocide;
             to give them serious consideration
             indicates no respect for human life.
FELIX   Enough!
JONATHAN   I will speak the truth.
FELIX   You shall not question my wisdom.
JONATHAN   The practice of murder is not wisdom.
FELIX   No more, I say. Leave my presence.
JONATHAN   I leave you now. But Judaea's suffering
             will rise from the stiffening corpses
             to puncture your dreams and haunt you forever.

Exit Jonathan.

FELIX   Those soft boys who pimp for Yahweh are blind.
             In the market babble reason's voice counts
             for nothing; only he who shouts is heard.
             And when I shout, it shall be with the sword.
             That such is needed I clearly see, Endor;
             but your tale of magic is new to me.
             This Simon Magus, the magician you named,
             is he known also by the name of Faust?
ENDOR   In Rome he has used that name.
FELIX   I know him. Popular report maintains
             in Laodicea once he challenged
             the local tribune, Faustus, for power,

and when his arrest was sought he transformed
the tribune's face into his own, ensuring,
in the confusion, his secure escape.
Since then common tongue has called him Faust.

ENDOR   Such tricks are typical of his magic.

FELIX   I hear also he can fly. Have any seen him?

AGRIPPA   None we know of.

FELIX   The man intrigues me. Where is he now?

ENDOR   He is in Jerusalem, and that which he failed to
achieve in Laodicea his magic would establish at
your expense.

FELIX   Are there any other magicians to back him?

ENDOR   Of lesser skill. He is the head; part him from the
body, and they cannot act.

FELIX   Has this magician troubled your reign, Agrippa?

AGRIPPA   He's from Samaria, not Judaea. I've heard of his
exploits elsewhere, no more.

FELIX   It's midnight, and we leave at dawn. We'll discuss
this more fully tomorrow.

Exeunt courtiers, musicians, soldiers.

FELIX   Brother, I anticipate your support in my efforts
to impress Roman law onto this agitated land.

AGRIPPA   I shall do what duty to kingship demands.

FELIX   Give me your arms, brother.

DRUSCILLA   Only your arms for me, Felix?

Druscilla kisses Felix.

FELIX   I trust you'll sleep well.

DRUSCILLA   Believe me, I shall scarcely sleep at all.

FELIX   Good night to you both.

Exeunt all but Felix and Marcus.

FELIX   Is all prepared to march at dawn?

MARCUS It is.

FELIX You will proceed us by one hour and in the market, the market you hear, not on any ground sanctified to Yahweh, you will place one Imperial Standard, defending it, if required, to the death.

MARCUS It is done.

FELIX And Marcus.

MARCUS Yes, excellency?

FELIX Let Jonathan re-enter Jerusalem, but I do not want to see him again, or hear his voice challenge my authority. Have I made myself understood?

Exeunt separately. Enter Agrippa and Endor.

AGRIPPA They are gone. Step through, old woman. Receive the due reward for your service.

ENDOR You found, then, my potion suited to your purpose?

AGRIPPA I have never seen a man so quickly enchanted, as Felix was with Druscilla. Your skill I acknowledge with gratitude. Yet I confess myself uneasy, too. What inspired you to talk of Simon Magus? I sought neither his inclusion tonight, nor approved his introduction to Felix.

ENDOR Inspiration controlled is not inspiration.

AGRIPPA He is nothing to anyone's purpose.

ENDOR I come as I am. Accept me for that, or acquire some other docile to your purposes, but devoid of true power.

AGRIPPA My sister comes. Leave us.

Enter Druscilla. Exit Endor.

DRUSCILLA Why talk to that hag? She makes my blood freeze.

AGRIPPA She impressed Felix. Through her we may find a¬way to move Felix in his policies.

DRUSCILLA Am I not influence enough?

AGRIPPA You've done well, and in so short a time.

DRUSCILLA I could do better.

AGRIPPA I'm sure of it. But to bed now; we wake early.

DRUSCILLA Brother.

AGRIPPA Yes, Druscilla.

DRUSCILLA I mean what I say.

AGRIPPA You do?

DRUSCILLA About Felix. I want to marry him.

AGRIPPA What?

DRUSCILLA I'm enchanted.

AGRIPPA Don't tell me you drank Felix's wine?

DRUSCILLA I drank only of his presence, and am now intoxicated.

AGRIPPA What of your husband?

DRUSCILLA He cares as little for me as I for him. We married only for convenience, to cement Emesa and Judaea in peace.

AGRIPPA It was from the Sanhedrin's impetus.

DRUSCILLA What they joined, they can put asunder. Surely, brother, you don't fear their objections?

AGRIPPA Your thought does not lack political weight. But let's not be precipitate. We shall see how this looks in the morning.

Exeunt.

♋ ♋ ♋

A bell, off. Enter leper.

LEPER Unclean! Unclean!

Enter Anan and Sapphira, with water.

SAPPHIRA Stop! Someone is here.

ANAN A leper. Old man, shift your gnarled bones. This

is no place for you. Deaf. No doubt half blind, too.

SAPPHIRA Elath! See what they've done! Do it yourself. I can't bear to look.

Anan moistens a cloth and attempts to give one of the crucified men to drink.

ANAN Calm yourself. He's too far gone to thirst.

SAPPHIRA I don't know who I weep most for: him or us. Anan, we should have given all the money from the sale of our possessions to the Nazoraeans, and not held back what we did.

ANAN But we decided together the Nazoraeans to-morrow could be crushed, and we would be left nothing. Holding back a little was only sensible.

SAPPHIRA I know. But I've been unable to sleep knowing we lied when we made our vows.

ANAN It's not too late. We could still return to Kepa and—

SAPPHIRA No, not Kepa. He's too harsh.

ANAN To Yacob, then. After all, we gave the money to him. We could do it tomorrow.

SAPPHIRA You think we should?

ANAN To speak the truth, my heart too has been troubled.

SAPPHIRA It's decided, then. I'm pleased. I feel much better already. Let's leave. There's nothing more we can do for Elath. Death has a terrible stench.

Enter Miryam, Thomas and Aaron. Exeunt Anan and Sapphira.

MIRYAM Jerusalem is so familiar, and yet its sights are all so unplaced, too. The Magus was right to suggest this walk. Each step says I lived here once, in my youth perhaps, when life made such strong impressions that no calamity could quite erase their marks. What place is this?

THOMAS The place of skulls.

AARON Where Jerusalem's crucifixions are done.

MIRYAM I—I—

AARON Miryam? Is she ill?

THOMAS She's remembering. Help her sit. These herbs will help her recover her breath.

AARON Do you know where you are?

MIRYAM I've been here—this hill—many years ago. I remember a crowd, the soldiers of Rome, and one man I loved hung, like those, up there. His groans—the blood—his last cry—

AARON Who was he?

MIRYAM I don't know. How could I not remember? His death was so terrible to witness. God! I suffered almost as much as he. No more; no more. Let's leave. I feel too much of something I don't understand.

Enter Zacharia.

ZACHARIA Here you are. This is no time for midnight walks.
I have news: Jerusalem mutters our
Magus today raised a girl from the dead.
The ignorant proclaim him Messiah;
the Sanhedrin is in apoplexy.
Reason says he should retire and allow
the general delusions to subside.
That way he might survive the month, at least.
Yet I have come from him just now, and he
declared not only his aversion to backing
from controversy, but his determination
to walk out tomorrow and confront the crowds.
I attempted to argue the point, show

	how he plays into the Sanhedrin's plans,
	but he is adamant: he'll walk the streets
	and bear whatever consequences may come.
THOMAS	I'm sure he has good reason.
ZACHARIA	He displayed none to me.
AARON	The Magus only acts with thought.
ZACHARIA	We each act only with thought. But some acts
	fit reason more nearly than do others.
AARON	You slur the Magus with such words.
ZACHARIA	I do not. His teaching is always to think
	and exercise our right to free-willed choice,
	accepting nothing but by our own regard.
	The Magus is no god; he makes mistakes.
	You'd do well to consider who serves him best
	the unthinking, accepting fool; or he
	who constantly questions all that is done.
	Frankly, I am disappointed in you.
	Your naivety, and your opposition
	to thought, offers Simon no protection.
	You cause me to feel I am alone.
THOMAS	Do you accept that the powers above
	guide us in our individual destinies?
ZACHARIA	Of course.
THOMAS	And they sort our lives to the good?
ZACHARIA	Naturally.
THOMAS	Then why interfere with their purposes?
ZACHARIA	When did the powers command we do nothing?
	You justify inaction as if it is to our glory. But
	rocks and stones are inactive, and they're used to
	execute dissenters. Refuse to act, and you exe-
	cute the Magus yourselves.
AARON	Let's not argue here. It's late, and Miryam re-
	quires rest. I do not yet know who is in the right,

but sleep is sure to clarify our thoughts and allow us tomorrow to decide.

THOMAS   We shall pray before sleep. If Zacharia proves
correct, we ourselves are unlikely to survive the
month either.

*Exeunt Miryam, Thomas, Aaron and Zacharia. The leper approaches
one of the crucified men, pulls off his shoulder cloth, stuffs it into his
bag, rings his bell.*

LEPER   Unclean! Unclean!

Exit leper.

♋   ♋   ♋

Enter Hebron and messenger.

HEBRON   Who called Agrippa our king? The man's a monster.
Jerusalem faces destruction, and all he thinks of
is his sister's marriage to our destroyer! What of
the standards? This says nothing of them.

MESSENGER   No addition accompanied the letter.

Enter Ananias.

HEBRON   Would Nero stand idly by and celebrate while
Rome burned? Yet that is what Agrippa would
do. Have you seen this?

ANANIAS   I ordered it brought to you.

HEBRON   And?

ANANIAS   This marriage suggestion intrigues me greatly.
Felix bound through Druscilla means our reach of
influence would strengthen immeasurably. There
is just one objection.

HEBRON   She is already married.

ANANIAS   A trifle. A marriage is easily annulled. Far more

serious is that Felix is uncircumcised, and as such must be unacceptable to Yahweh. We need, somehow, to circumcise him.

Enter Mordecai.

HEBRON   When? While he saunas? Or should we slice him as he sleeps? Really, Ananias, I feel you are over-simplifying the situation. Judaea's future scarcely dangles on a Roman foreskin.

ANANIAS   Yahweh works in mysterious ways. What news?

MORDECAI   None yet of Felix, or his standards. But I have our witnesses ready.

ANANIAS   Bring them in.

Mordecai signals. Guards bring in Joel and Adina.

ANANIAS   Our plans against Simon Magus proceed. Two of his former disciples, sickened by his magical perversions, have volunteered to testify before the tribunal.

MORDECAI   Acknowledge your head priest.

HEBRON   What troubles them?

MORDECAI   They're terrified we're going to kill them.

ANANIAS   My friends, we appreciate your assistance in this. Be assured, no harm will come to you. As Yahweh's hand in Judaea, you have my word.

Enter messenger.

HEBRON   They don't look material conducive to our plans.

MORDECAI   When the time comes they'll talk, believe me.

ANANIAS   Speak.

MESSENGER   Simon Magus has entered the streets. The crowd calls him rabbi, and Messiah.

ANANIAS   I'll speak again to these later. Take them away. Mordecai, observe the Magus. If he blasphemes, so much closer to our purpose. You: I want to be informed immediately Felix or his standards are sighted. Go!

Exeunt severally.

   ♋   ♋   ♋

Enter Simon Magus, Miryam, Thomas, Aaron, Zacharia and a crowd of Jerusalem's citizens. Simon blesses those in the crowd, one by one.

ZACHARIA   Stand back! You'll trample the Magus with your jostling. Be patient. Each will be blessed. In a line. Idiot! Do you not know obedience is the first virtue?

CITIZEN 9   Did you hear? Some say Simon Magus is the Messiah.

CITIZEN 10   How can he be? He's not descended from the house ¬of David.

CITIZEN 9   Frankly, I don't care if his father climbed over the back fence. If he can act for us against the Romans, I'm for him to the end.

Enter girl. Enter Mordecai.

CROWD   That's the child the Magus raised from the dead.—Doesn't she look well?—She looks like death to me.—Well, considering what she's been through.—Make way!—Poor thing.—Let her through!

GIRL   Magus, I come at my father's bidding.
He gave me this to present to you.
I don't know why, for yesterday I was sick.
They say I died almost, but for a miracle.

SIMON   Who says this, daughter?

GIRL   My mother, and my grandfather.

	My father would too, but it's blasphemy;
	only Yahweh has the power to save.
SIMON	And what do you say?
GIRL	I know only I was sick, but after
	my father spoke with you, I recovered.
	If your power cured me, my family
	and I in gratitude offer you this.
	If not, please pass it on to that which did.
SIMON	Daughter, you are welcome.
	Go back now to your family's comfort;
	you do yourself much good by your courage.
	Take my blessings with you.
GIRL	Thank you, Magus. Thank you.

Exit girl.

MORDECAI	Rabbi, hear my plea for help.
SIMON	Who calls me rabbi?
MORDECAI	I do.
SIMON	Shrug the crowd's protection. I am no rabbi.
MORDECAI	Forgive me. I'm flustered. My mother is dying,
	and the physicians are unable to cure her.
	You are my last hope; please don't deny me.
SIMON	Why should I help you?
MORDECAI	You have the power to do miracles.
SIMON	I have?
ZACHARIA	Who is this man? I think he means to trap you.
SIMON	Let him have his say.
MORDECAI	You saved that girl by miracle.
SIMON	I never said so.
MORDECAI	They do.
SIMON	But they saw nothing.
	What proof of miracle do you possess?
MORDECAI	Yesterday she was dying; now she is well.
SIMON	Each day hundreds recover from illness.

	Am I responsible for them all?
MORDECAI	You deny, then, a miracle by your hand
	saved that girl from certain death?
SIMON	My hand lives at my hand's extremity;
	the girl you saw lives across the city.
	How could my hand have been involved?
MORDECAI	Then why accept the girl's gratitude?
SIMON	I have not: it was passed on to that power
	by which the cure was effected.
MORDECAI	What power is that?
SIMON	You have so little faith, you do not know?
MORDECAI	You deliberately misconstrue my meaning.
SIMON	I doubt you know yourself your own meaning.
MORDECAI	My meaning is plain: did you, or did you not,
	by miracle, redeem that girl from death?
SIMON	You place a burden on the miraculous
	that it has never existed to bear.
	To search for miracles is natural
	in peoples downtrodden and despairing;
	it provides their one hope for salvation.
	But is not life itself the miracle
	the fact we live, breathe, and grow to wisdom;
	the which to ignore by specious gropings
	after the miraculous indicates
	only spiritual immaturity,
	for nothing obtains from nothing, and such
	miracles as you seek must, finally,
	count in the spiritual realm as nothing.
MORDECAI	Magus, you spit on Yahweh Sabaoth.
	The flight of the angel at Passover;
	Egypt's destruction by fever and plague;
	Moses, raised in his enemy's house,
	stopping the Red Sea; in the wilderness

finding mana; bringing back from Sinai
the commandments etched in stone
these miracles Judaea was born from,
they are the rock upon which our people grows.
By miracles Yahweh loves us, guides us,
renews his covenant with us, his chosen.
How can so much be accounted nothing?
May Yahweh cut off any who dare so speak!

SIMON   A faith resting on exaggerations
of hundreds of years ago is, at best,
insipid; at worst, usurpation of reason.
Perhaps these fantasies truly occurred;
I wasn't there. But history and myth
are close relations, and as time passes
each becomes the other, entangled in
ways too few prove inclined to separate.

MORDECAI   Our scriptures and prophets do so for us,
inspired by Yahweh's loving providence.

SIMON   The body is earth, the spirit fire
their impulses are alien, opposed.
Neither spirit is known through the body,
nor are earthly miracles spiritual.
Fools weigh their wisdom by fleshly proofs,
but to seek the spiritual sensually is
ignorance, not wisdom. It can't be so found.

MORDECAI   You hypocrite, Simon Magus! You preach
of the spirit, but consort with prostitutes.

SIMON   Who, my friend, is the prostitute here?

MORDECAI   She is. The whore your pupils try to hide.
Observe this woman! Examine her face!
Are not the lineaments of lust creased
deep around her eyes? She is Helena,
and comes from Tyre, where for twenty years

[68]

she has plied her sinful occupation.
This foul creature, people of Jerusalem,
Simon, the Magus, proclaims his angel;
in Tyre he bragged he raised her from the dead.
This is the liar you call Messiah!

SIMON You speak the words of others, not mine.

MORDECAI Tell us, then, Messiah, why this prostitute
has become your necessary consort?

SIMON I consort with truth, and raise the fallen.

MORDECAI You consort with Beelzebub, and use magic
to mislead the foolish into evil.

ZACHARIA Mind your speech. You are not among friends
here.

CROWD Who is this fool?—No friend of mine.—But
everyone knows the Samaritan is a magician.—
At least he helps us, which is more than the
Temple priests offer.—Magus! Magus! Magus!
Magus! Magus!

SIMON Silence! Friend, answer me but one question.
You asked me to cure your sick mother.

MORDECAI What of it?

SIMON Speak the truth you hold so dear, and tell all
here how it is you have thirteen mothers.

MORDECAI I don't know of what you speak.

SIMON So quickly truth becomes victim to policy.

MORDECAI He's mad! Possessed by Beelzebub utterly!

Marching, off.

CROWD Soldiers!—Break it up—Quick! Before they get
here!

SIMON Return to your mothers, friend. Their illness
is ignorance, of which they won't be cured.
Exeunt the crowd and Mordecai.

AARON   Of what mothers do you speak?

SIMON   The Sanhedrin: he is their extension.
But other matters more concern us now.
Listen closely. Inside the next two days
the sun here will suffer a total eclipse,
completing one cycle, beginning the next.
Knowing this, my teacher's duty compels me
to initiate you remaining three,
and Miryam, our newly-found sister,
into the mystery my teaching has,
these eight years past, progressed you each towards.
Once done you will be free to choose your
course.
Meet hence at my house in one hour's time.
There I shall both instruct and farewell you.
Come Miryam. Beware of Rome's sentries.

Exeunt Simon and Miryam.

ZACHARIA   What meaning is there in this?

AARON   It's unanticipated news to me. Thomas?

THOMAS   I think it is what he said: the end.

ZACHARIA   Not if I am still alive, it isn't.
The Sanhedrin threatens Simon with death.
So much is clear. What is still to be discerned
is how far we may yet divert their plans.
I propose we see the Sanhedrin ourselves
and question them regarding their purpose.
It may be we can disabuse them of doubts
they have relevant to Simon's motives,
and save the Magus from their reprisals.

AARON   You assume the Magus lacks acumen.

ZACHARIA   I assume nothing. But who else will act for him?

THOMAS   I cannot support you, Zacharia.

ZACHARIA Why not?

THOMAS We have discussed this already. The Sanhedrin's
purpose is political, not spiritual.
They are more likely to extinguish your light,
than suffer illumination by yours.

ZACHARIA Aaron, what of you?

AARON Thomas is right. You are no Daniel that
you should survive such a lion's den as theirs.

ZACHARIA I'm disappointed. I expected more of you both.

AARON We shall pray for you.

ZACHARIA Pray for yourselves, to learn courage.

THOMAS Shalom, brother.

Exeunt Thomas and Aaron.

ZACHARIA I don't know who here will prove justified.
But it's better to act than do nothing at all.

Exit Zacharia.

♋   ♋   ♋

Enter Jonathan, Lysias and soldiers. Enter spy, separately.

LYSIAS What news, then, of Antonius Felix?

JONATHAN He's determined to march standards into Jerusalem.

LYSIAS He wants to walk a carpet of bleeding bodies.
You've informed him of the consequences?

JONATHAN I have.

LYSIAS Who has he to arrange this lunacy?

JONATHAN Marcus. You know him?

LYSIAS A most efficient soldier, and sure to fully implement
Felix's demands. How far is Marcus behind you?

JONATHAN An hour, at most.

LYSIAS I need to prepare my men if a massacre is to be
averted. What does the Sanhedrin know?

JONATHAN It has its spies. No doubt Ananias has been informed.

LYSIAS That King Agrippa accompanies Felix I doubt can be a blessing. The populace is impressed by neither his wealth nor his swish. If Felix wants history to remember him, he has set himself an indelible course. Where do you now go?

JONATHAN To ready myself. The populace is sure to be incensed. Someone is required to take the lead ¬and divert it from the extremity of violence towards some stance less likely to end in slaughter.

LYSIAS Attempt that, and you have my powers of backing.

JONATHAN Thank you, Lysias. I'm pleased you have the ration of reason your procurator lacks.

LYSIAS Get this behind us, and we'll see where else our co-operation may lead.

Exeunt.

♋ ♋ ♋

Ananias and Hebron enter, accompanied by spy. Mordecai and Zach-aria enter separately.

HEBRON My information is accurate. Jonathan plots with Lysias to replace you as head priest. It is probable he visited Antonius Felix to further cement his position with the Roman administration, ensur-ing his support over yours.

ANANIAS Jonathan must die.

HEBRON How? Even we cannot kill a former head priest without drawing attention to our involvement.

ANANIAS A means has already presented itself. Mordecai, bring us the magician's puppy. Maintain then the watch for Felix and his standards. *(To Hebron)* Watch now, and wonder. What is his name?

MORDECAI   Zacharia.

ANANIAS   Zacharia. Step forwards.

Exit Mordecai.

ZACHARIA   Thank you, Ananias, for seeing me. I come to assure you—

ANANIAS   I know why you are here. You want us to forget the blasphemies of Simon Magus, his preaching of a power alternative to Yahweh, and his stirring of the populace against our authority. You ask a great deal. Tell me: you know the teaching of Moses which commands an eye for an eye, a tooth for a tooth? That is what we require. In exchange for the life of Simon Magus, we desire a life from you.

ZACHARIA   You gladly have mine in exchange for that of the Magus.

ANANIAS   Don't misunderstand me. Not yours. Another's.

ZACHARIA   Whose?

ANANIAS   Jonathan.

ZACHARIA   You want me to murder the former head priest?

ANANIAS   We want you to prosecute Yahweh's will.

ZACHARIA   And if I do it you guarantee Simon Magus may leave Jerusalem untouched and free?

ANANIAS   You have my word.

ZACHARIA   It's more than I anticipated. To kill a human being is no easy task.

ANANIAS   We are not negotiable.

ZACHARIA   May I consider it?

ANANIAS   Return your answer here in one hour, or we shall proceed against the magician.

ZACHARIA   Shalom.

Exit Zacharia.

HEBRON   It's an admirable solution. But will he do it?

ANANIAS   What choice does he have?

Enter Mordecai.

MORDECAI   The standards are seen, one hour from Jerusalem.

ANANIAS   Yahweh surely guides us. Both Jonathan and Simon Magus shall die today, and at a single stroke. Come. I'll tell you of my plan.

Exeunt.

♋   ♋   ♋

Enter Simon Magus, Miryam, Thomas and Aaron.

SIMON   Where is Zacharia?

AARON   Not yet returned.

SIMON   You two have prepared yourselves?

THOMAS   We've been at prayer this hour past.

SIMON   Good. We shall make a start.

Enter Zacharia.

ZACHARIA   Magus, forgive me my lateness. I was detained.

SIMON   You detain yourself, Zacharia.

ZACHARIA   Do you chastise me?

SIMON   No, brother, I would not influence you.
Your right to choice must be respected.
But consider well, for your decision
determines your fate only, none else's.
Yet this is from our immediate purpose.
We shall talk now of why you are.
I earlier said an eclipse tomorrow
ends one cycle and issues in the next.

This fact demands my last act towards you,
my disciples, be one of confirmation
in the mysteries I, to date, have taught.
That I now do. This world is filled with gods.
Greece has Zeus, Persia Ahura Mazdah,
Egypt the ever-present Amen-Ra,
each nation else its own guardian gods
which, through a lesser pantheon, rewards
and punishes those who crave their guidance.
In Judaea here Yahweh fills that function.
And this I say is good for, whether real
or imagined, these gods imbue in worshippers
doubt, that we are of petty significance.
And yet, despite their holy exercises,
these pious are ignorant too; for there
exists another god, incomprehensible,
so deep and vast it is unknown to all.
This god's a power of immeasurable light,
a Fire burning in the midst of silence,
the ultimate mover of earthly existence
yet inaccessible to the earthly senses.
So great is this Fire, so intense its being,
that none can see it directly; the shock
would obliterate their shuddering soul.
Thus there exists a spiritual order
whereby what we cannot bear naked descends
through an intermediate hierarchy,
to end clothed in the flesh of suns and stars,
whose physical light but reflects that Fire
which filters down from the regions above.
And herein resides the secret of life.
For if Fire above descended below,
so a path exists from the sensual

creation back to the spiritual source,
and this fleshly encasement is not our end,
but a springboard rather from which we may,
in love, rebound to that from which we came.
Only then does the unknown God manifest,
and the hidden Fire stand revealed.
Knowing that Fire, to the degree permitted,
is the sole intent of all my teaching.
And in that knowledge I would initiate
you remaining four. What are your questions?

AARON You said four? Is Miryam one of us now?

SIMON She is.

AARON I mean no disrespect: I love Miryam
as I would a sister. But for eight years
we have faithfully practised your teaching,
while Miryam has been with you merely months.
How, then, is she of equal placement to us?

SIMON Sometimes the first are last, the last first.

AARON I don't understand.

SIMON Your time for understanding has not yet come.

ZACHARIA I think, perhaps, he misstated his case.
What Aaron desired to say, but could not,
is our loved sister was a prostitute.
We do not judge her for that; destiny
sometimes places us where we would rather not be.
Yet you teach us the necessity of virtue,
that sin might not profane our purity.
So how, then, is Miryam one of us?

SIMON Who are you to judge who's pure and who is not?
Inward, not outward, attributes matter
one lives perversely, but grace arrives and
lifts her into holiness; another
prays zealously, yet his heart remains cold.

Cause and effect acts lawfully here below;
but on what Fire touches, laws cease to act.
If this was not so we would be trapped in flesh,
encased forever in our sensual selves,
with never any hope for liberation.

MIRYAM   Brothers, I understand your confusion,
for it is equally my own. I owe
the Magus even more than do you three,
my life since he saved me having transformed
so much for the better that when I wake
each morning I scarcely recognise myself,
nor cannot believe I am no longer
the self-pitying, disgusting woman
I, so few months ago, was. If this change
confuses you, it fills me with amazement
and gratitude, that the little I am
should be the recipient of so much.

SIMON   Thomas, you have a question? Voice it.

THOMAS   How do we unveil the hidden Fire?

SIMON   Fire exists in silence: that I have said.
Be silent yourself, and all is revealed.
What other questions do you have for me?
Kneel then. We shall pray and learn the truth.

The five kneel and pray in silence.

SIMON   Will no-one stay awake with me?

ZACHARIA   I don't sleep.

AARON   Neither do I.

They resume silent prayer.

SIMON   I said, will none stay awake with me?

ZACHARIA   I am awake.

AARON   As am I.

They resume silent prayer. Light, above. An angel appears above, descends, touches first Miryam then Thomas on the top of the head, ascends, disappears. Shouting, off. The light fades. All stand, severally.

ZACHARIA   Trouble.

SIMON   It's not our concern. Zacharia, Aaron, I suggest you leave for Idumaea, where brothers and sisters I hold dear shall instruct you where I am no longer able.

ZACHARIA   Why must we go elsewhere?

SIMON   You are not yet ripened.

ZACHARIA   But you need us here.

SIMON   I do not force you: the choice remains yours. I say it only to assist your growth.

ZACHARIA   I would not be so selfish as to worry of myself when you stand so near danger.

SIMON   So you will not leave Jerusalem?

ZACHARIA   No.

SIMON   Aaron? Would you stay too?

AARON   I shall take your advice and go.

SIMON   The sooner the better. Come, brother. I'll give you letters and food. Miryam will teach you the way.

Exeunt Simon, Miryam and Aaron. The shouting becomes louder.

ZACHARIA   Who told the Magus I saw the Sanhedrin?

THOMAS   No-one. There has been no time.

ZACHARIA   Do you still maintain we should do nothing to help him?

THOMAS   He has not sought our assistance.

ZACHARIA   How can he? He's dependent on us thinking for ourselves and acting then as we see fit. Thomas, how far would you proceed to save Simon? Would you sacrifice a life?

THOMAS   My own, you mean?

ZACHARIA   Let's say your own.

THOMAS   If it was required, yes. But that is not yet needed, surely?

ZACHARIA   I meant what I said to the Magus just now. I care nothing for myself nor for my own closeness to the Fire. He is the one with the powers; he is the one whom the lost world needs. In order to extend his life, I will do whatever I must.

THOMAS   What does the Sanhedrin require of you?

ZACHARIA   And I thought you naive. Brother, embrace me. Don't worry. I shall leave Jerusalem soon enough. Remember me in your prayers.

Exeunt separately.

♋   ♋   ♋

Enter Ananias and Mordecai. Shouting off, louder.

ANANIAS   Tell me what the Romans are doing.

MORDECAI   Marching.

ANANIAS   How many standards do they carry?

MORDECAI   Just the one.

ANANIAS   Raised or lowered?

MORDECAI   Raised.

ANANIAS   And the mob?

MORDECAI   So far the Romans have avoided sanctified ground.

ANANIAS   Let's hope they continue to do so. Otherwise a blood-bath will be inevitable. Keep me informed.

Enter Hebron and Zacharia. Exit Mordecai.

ANANIAS   So, my friend, will you do it?

ZACHARIA   Will you guarantee freedom for Simon Magus if I do?

ANANIAS   He may leave Jerusalem untouched.

ZACHARIA I am your servant.

Enter Mordecai.

MORDECAI The Romans have entered the market square. A large crowd goes to meet them, with Jonathan at its head.

ANANIAS Now is our chance. Hebron, take Zacharia and brief him.

Exeunt Hebron and Zacharia.

MORDECAI Allow me to back him. If he fails, I'll do the assassination myself, then secret the dagger on his person.

ANANIAS We can't lose. This day will prove Judaea's glory.

Exeunt.

♋   ♋   ♋

Enter Roman soldiers led by Marcus. One of them carries an Imperial Standard. A chanting crowd follows, Jonathan leading them.

CROWD Freedom! Freedom! Freedom!

JONATHAN My fathers, my brothers, my brothers' sons;
silence your indignation and hear me speak.
You all know my name. I am Jonathan,
once head priest of the Temple, today reduced
to stature equivalent to your own.
Yet Yahweh never forgets those he has raised,
nor do those servants unlearn the wisdom
position and privilege has taught them.
Duty compels me to share that wisdom with you.
But allow me first to pose a question.
Who rules in Jerusalem here? We Jews?

CROWD No!

JONATHAN King Agrippa, then?

CROWD   No!—He's nothing!—He's just a puppet!

JONATHAN   So it must be the Sanhedrin.

CROWD   They do nothing.—They only do what they're told!

JONATHAN   Who then? The procurator?

CROWD   Yes!—The procurator!—He's the one who rules!

JONATHAN   But who appointed Antonius Felix
and those procurators which preceded him?

CROWD   Rome!—They're our enemies!—We are ruled by Rome!

Enter Agrippa, Lysias and Felix. The crowd jeers them.

JONATHAN   Silence, people! You have touched our troubles'
pulse.
Rome rules us. Rome and the principals of Rome.
Yet to what good is this rule directed?
We have the procurator's words in answer:
this rule is to enhance great Rome's glory.
And, he says, Rome's glory is also our own.
Who cares if we lose our freedom, for we
have gained an empire; why desire a voice
when great Caesar speaks the good for us all?
Forget that when Rome was but a savage tribe,
scratching under a midnight moon, this world's
ruler led our fathers to sanctuary.
For those savages are men now, good men,
who know equally what is for our good.
Just because great Nero in Rome tortured
to death his wife, mother and brother, hanging
their naked corpses in the common market
for beggars to spit upon and vilify,
do not think he's lost his pulse of goodness.
He has not! Indeed, he thinks so highly

of Judaea's ancient pedigree that,
in his knowing estimation, only
former slaves stand high enough to rule us now.

Enter Ananias and Hebron. Enter Zacharia and Mordecai, separately.

JONATHAN Neither lament the taxes we're levied,
for they support Caesar; and though at times
froth attends his speech, yet Nero's a good man.
As are all the men who assist Rome's rule.
Ananias, Hebron, the Sadducees
and its supporters—they are good men all.
Brothers, embrace the troops marching our streets,
for they are here to make us civilised.
If your daughter falls bloodied through the door,
raped by a drunken cohort on pay night,
it's a small price for being civilised.
Neither allow your gut to feel the nail
driven through your son's clenched wrist; the
thick blood
congealing on each barb of Caesar's rule
is good, and in a world where we are slaves
those shafts of goodness are as miracles
for which we must give Rome our grateful thanks.
Because it is for our good that this is done.

CROWD Kill them!—Kill them all!—Freedom! Freedom!
Freedom!

AGRIPPA Jerusalem!

ANANIAS Jerusalem, allow your king to speak.

CROWD He's no king of ours!—He's Caesar's toy!—Freedom! Freedom! Freedom!

ANANIAS In the name of Yahweh and Yahweh's council,
I command you hear my holy office!

CROWD Silence!—Let him speak!—Give the dog rope to
hang himself with!

ANANIAS   I know not all here respect another's view,
for we argue to persuade, not to be persuaded.
Yet give your good king, Agrippa, his due.
Many times he has defended your rights;
allow him now the right he owns to speak.

AGRIPPA   Jerusalem, what I would have say is brief.
In truth, I do not speak at all except
I know you are not unanimous for revolt.
Young men, to you rebellion's a game,
so naturally you pant for Roman blood.
But your elders remember stiff corpses
set in lines beneath Jerusalem's walls,
and the all-night fires to warm the wailing
women whose cries sent shivers among the stars.
It is folly to seek that time again;
Rome is with us, and we must live with her.
The time to fight was eighty years ago,
when Pompey invaded Jerusalem.
Then we were a powerful people, and free.
Yet our forefathers, with all their resources,
fell to a mere fraction of Rome's army.
How then will you, with no resources at all
but bare hands, bravery, and blood, vanquish
the combined might of the Roman Empire?
To dream of victory is foolishness.
So do not blame Rome for your slavery;
blame your own ancestors who failed at war,
then bred their caged children to servitude.
For you are all slaves, the children of slaves.
I know you citizens are offended
by the standard Felix ordered placed here,
that you think Yahweh disapproves its presence.
Yet this too is folly, for how could Rome

have built so vast an Empire if Yahweh
himself had not approved her advances?
And before you decide to rebel, further
consider the religious consequences.
Custom demands you cease war each Sabbath;
yet that is when Pompey crushed our fathers,
by thrusting most when they were worshipping.
But transgress Yahweh's law by fighting, and
what is left to fight for? Yahweh ignored
is your sole reason for war abandoned.
Jerusalem, revolt has but one end.
Far wiser to kill outright your own wives
and children, consigning this wondrous land
to flames, for by such lunacy at least
the shame of defeat would be avoided.
I know folly is preferred to wisdom,
that blood heated is always slow to cool.
Yet act rightly now and not only you
have my blessings, but the solace of peace;
however, follow your passions and you walk
without me to inevitable doom.
Consider carefully before you act.

ANANIAS My brothers, my sons, I know how you feel.
Death seems attractive when your life is hell.
But no death, however glorious and brave,
justifies our Holy Temple's outrage.
We may now be slaves, yet our Temple is intact;
rebel, and even that comfort is lost us.
In the name of Yahweh Sabaoth and his
great angels in heaven, forget your pain.
Go home. Let our sacred Temple still stand.

CROWD He's right.—He's lying to save himself!—Let's
turn back.—Stay here and we die!

JONATHAN Brothers! Are these the voices of Judaea?
          Did Yahweh release us from Egypt's yoke
          to live beneath a Roman blasphemy?
   CROWD No!—Never!—We want freedom!
JONATHAN Bring down the corpses.

Several from the crowd begin lowering the crucified men.

JONATHAN Let us remember why we are here.
          Rome has always allowed us our worship,
          and respected the form our worship takes.
          Now Antonius Felix, Nero's slave,
          wishes to besmirch that pledge and shoulder
          Nero's face through Jerusalem's holy streets.
          Its ugliness itself offends, without
          the insult to Yahweh and Judaea.
          We speak now not revolt, but the holding
          to a promise Rome has already made.
          Our subject's right is to worship Yahweh
          in his duly consecrated Temple,
          unmolested by boyish brinkmanship.
          Forget the head priest's servile excuses
          how can our heritage be further raped
          when such rights are spat back into our faces?
          Jerusalem, these corpses testify
          our commitment to peace: we sacrifice
          our children to pacify Roman law.
          And what does Caesar offer in exchange?
          A procurator buoyed by disrespect,
          whose first act in Judaea is sacrilege.
          There can be no excuses, so hear none.
          Antonius Felix! We have signed in blood
          our acquiescence to Rome's authority.
          Will you, in turn, discharge your obligations
          and remove this insult from Yahweh's ground?

FELIX   Accept Caesar's image, or suffer the sword.

JONATHAN   Jerusalem, bow down! Bend your necks to destiny!

The crowd bows. Enter Simon and Thomas. They bow with the rest.

JONATHAN   We are immovable. We do not revolt;
but we shall never accept Nero's image.
It offends Yahweh, sickens honesty,
and betrays the tenets of Roman justice.
Kill us if you will. Yet we'll remain here
until all standards from Jerusalem are gone.

Jonathan bows with the rest.

FELIX   Can they be serious?

LYSIAS   Unfortunately, yes.

FELIX   This is preposterous. In no other land would such lunacy prevail.

LYSIAS   Judaea is like no other land.

FELIX   Agrippa, can't you move them?

AGRIPPA   I'm only their king. You see that means nothing here.

ANANIAS   Permit me to speak. I am Ananias, Jerusalem's head priest. Once before this occurred, in King Herod's time. Then, as now, the crowd's intent was unchangeable. Yet there exists a way to turn this provocation to triumph, and have the crowd singing your praises.

FELIX   I am listening.

ANANIAS   They will not withdraw. Therefore your choice is simple: to massacre, or to forgive. But if you massacre you can't just kill one or two, you'll need to kill thousands, so primed is this city by frustration and despair.

FELIX   A few thousand Jews less makes no difference to me. Tell me why it should.

ANANIAS	For reputation and respect.
FELIX	If I back down the crowd's acclamation will go to Jonathan, surely?
ANANIAS	I can guarantee it won't.
FELIX	You can? Why do so?
ANANIAS	I seek my place in power as much as you. Allow me to exercise my position in this, and your rule here is assured a popular foundation. For as you prosper, so do we. Should I fail, the sword is always available after.
JONATHAN	Procurator, your decision! Life? Or death?
FELIX	Jerusalem! Your attachment to a god which has¬ deserted you is foolish; but I admire your fervour. I seek nothing but respect for Rome. Do I have your commitment to that?
CROWD	Yes!—You do!—You do!
FELIX	Put up your swords. Cover the standard and remove it from the city.
HEBRON	Long live the procurator!
CROWD	Long live Antonius Felix!

The crowd stands, sings a hymn to Yahweh. A scream. The singing stops, the crowd parts. Jonathan has been stabbed. Zacharia stands beside him, knife in hand. Mordecai grabs Zacharia. Jonathan falls.

MORDECAI	Murder! Murder!
CROWD	Kill him! Kill him!
LYSIAS	Protect the assassin from the crowd.

Soldiers approach Zacharia, take him from Mordecai.

ANANIAS	Jerusalem! Look now upon the corpse of greatness and surrender your anger. This is a time for love, not for vengeance. Jonathan is dead, but his ideal lives on. You each heard Jonathan's speech today.

He sought peace with Rome, not rebellion;
an honourable acceptance of our fate.
Refuse the lead of those his murderers
who respect neither Judaea nor Rome
in their quest for Jerusalem's destruction;
rather respect Jonathan's memory, and obey.
Antonius Felix, your magnanimity
proves yourself our friend, and no tormenter.
As honourableness demands fealty,
so you have the Sanhedrin's hand, and mine.
Leave to us this swine: our Law will dispose
his sin according to ancient prescription.
Concede this single request and receive
our praises. Long live Antonius Felix!

CROWD Long live Antonius Felix!—Felix!—Felix!—Felix!

ANANIAS Jerusalem, you deal yourself justly
by accepting the procurator thus.
It signals the peace which Jonathan sought.
Let us then respect his death and disperse
ourselves, content no other blood is shed.
Take him away.

SIMON Halt!

ANANIAS Who dares order me?

SIMON I do, Simon of Samaria.

CROWD Stand back!—Let him through!

ANANIAS Magician, what would you say?

SIMON Murder needs a corpse. But this man is alive.

CROWD Let him through!

Simon and Thomas approach Jonathan. Simon takes a bag off Thomas, takes out leaves, crushes them, combines them with spittle, and places them on the wound. Jonathan revives. Thomas helps him stand.

CROWD A miracle!—Jerusalem, the Messiah has come —
The Messiah has come!

HEBRON   Blasphemy!

FELIX   Lysias, have the magician arrested.

Lysias signals. The centurion and several soldiers make towards Simon and Thomas. The crowd closes ranks, preventing the soldiers from reaching them. Others in the crowd help Jonathan.

FELIX   I want the magician.

CROWD   Magus! Magus! Magus!

Protected by the crowd, Simon and Thomas exit. Mordecai exits with Zacharia.

FELIX   Enough. Clear the streets!

The centurion signals the soldiers, who push the chanting crowd off.

FELIX   Ananias, you say this city is yours. Bring me the magician.

Exeunt all but Ananias and Hebron.

ANANIAS   Magus, you are dead!

Exeunt.

♋   ♋   ♋

Enter Miryam and Aaron.

MIRYAM   You understand the paths you must follow?

AARON   I do.

MIRYAM   The Magus requested you pass on this letter to Dositheus upon arrival. It will guarantee your acceptance into his school, and communicate to our brothers and sisters what has occurred here. Aaron, I've known you only a short time, but you will be missed. You tremble.

AARON   I'm ashamed. Miryam, beside you I am only a child. Forgive me, please.

MIRYAM   Hush. Nothing to forgive; nothing to forgive.

AARON   I hope we meet again, yet something in me fears
we won't. I'll remember you always.

Enter Thomas.

MIRYAM   Where is Zacharia?

THOMAS   Detained by orders of the Sanhedrin. The Magus
himself has just escaped the admiring crowds and
waits nearby. He says, Miryam, there is one more
you must meet if your memory is to recover. That
meeting he would establish now. Thomas, time
runs against us. Come now to farewell the Magus,
then I'll accompany you to Jerusalem's outskirts.
Come dusk, all must be resolved.

Exeunt.

♋   ♋   ♋

Enter Kepa and Yacob.

KEPA   Yacob, we have remained companions, holding
master Yeshu's torch for twenty-five years now,
respecting each the other's position,
in tandem giving our brethren to suck.
I love and admire you your wisdom;
after Yeshu you stand first in my heart.
But, brother, I warn you: do not cross me.
I'll brook no compromise of the Word.

YACOB   What compromise? I suggest only—

KEPA   The compromise you have already made.

YACOB   No, Kepa; for once your tongue has crucified
the truth. I act in this only from compassion.
Anan and Sapphira regret their lapse;
it is for us now to reaccept them,
forgiveness being the loving solution.
I do not see such as compromise at all.

KEPA   Yacob, your ignorance amazes me.
        Must I again repeat: we are besieged
        and cannot afford sentimentality.
        If we allow this couple forgiveness
        we provocate dissension for ourselves
        where is obedience to our vows, where
        discipline, if wanderers are not rebuked?
        We are few; our one hope for survival
        rests in unity: unity proceeds all.

YACOB   You take an overly harsh perspective.
        Yeshu always said we must turn the cheek
        and accept our brethren for what they are.

KEPA   You throw Yeshu in my face? Hypocrite!
        Who considered Yeshu mad, and refused
        to support him even in his own village?
        While I slept three years in fields and caves,
        starving at times because I—I!—had faith
        that revelation spoke through his doings!
        Remember, Yacob, Yeshu named me his Rock,
        upon whom the Word's purity depends.
        You may be Yeshu's brother, but I, of all,
        am the one confidante to Yeshu's soul.
        So do not counsel me on what Yeshu
        did or did not say. I was there; I know!
        They come. Calm yourself. I shall administer
        this not according to my emotion,
        but by what we Nazoraeans require.

*Enter Sapphira, Anan, Zebah and other Nazoraeans. Enter Simon and
Miryam, unseen.*

KEPA   Brothers, sisters, Shalom. Each day we are one is
        another to Yahweh's glory. Anan, you have some-
        thing to tell us.

ANAN   I do. Sapphira and I—we do not possess the strength others have been granted. When we broke bread among you Nazoraeans our hearts did not follow what our lips promised. That now has changed. In sorrow and anguish we reaffirm our pledge to Yeshu's teaching, and submit ourselves to your re-acceptance.

SAPPHIRA   Amen.

KEPA   Well?

SAPPHIRA   We don't understand.

KEPA   Is that all you have to say?

SAPPHIRA   It's all Yacob instructed us to speak.

KEPA   Anan, do you recognise this?

ANAN   It's a bag. It was mine.

KEPA   And what did it contain?

ANAN   Talents.

KEPA   These talents?

ANAN   Perhaps. All coins look the same when—

KEPA   To whom were these talents consigned?

ANAN   To you. And to Jerusalem's faithful.

KEPA   Wrong! They are for Yahweh. Anan, tell me; did not you and I have an agreement? Weren't you to sell your land and possessions then donate the proceeds to Yeshu's mission? Isn't that what you, Sapphira and I agreed?

ANAN   Yes.

KEPA   Speak louder. Not all can hear.

ANAN   Yes.

KEPA   How then could Satan have so possessed your souls that you could lie to the Holy Spirit and retain coins for your snivelling selves?

ANAN   Forgive us.

KEPA   What?

SAPPHIRA	He said, forgive us.
KEPA	Forgive you? How? When it is not to us that you have lied, but to Yahweh in heaven? When not your brothers and sisters are betrayed, but your own putrid souls in Yahweh's sight?
SAPPHIRA	We weren't sure. Jerusalem is boiling. You, Yacob, all here might be dead tomorrow. So we held back a little. Just in case.
ANAN	It was for safety, not insult.
SAPPHIRA	We meant no harm.
ANAN	Yacob, father. You understand our motives.
YACOB	Kepa is our fulcrum here. Obey his wisdom.
KEPA	And I will stand no argument.

You of little faith, these are the last days;
we prepare for Yeshu's return when, wearing
the Messiah's crown, he rewards all those
who have kept his Word, and punishes the rest.
Of what use will be your gold talents then?
That you followed Anan's initiatives
I understand: a loving wife obeys
her husband's dictates, whether right or wrong.
So it is from Anan we must procure
suitable endorsement on Yahweh's behalf.
Zebah, accompany Anan inside.
On the table of his heart he shall lay
his despicable soul's quiverings, from which
Yahweh shall choose acceptance or rejection.
Go now.

Exit Anan, followed by Zebah and one other.

KEPA	While Anan prays for his future within, silent vigil shall be our course out here.

All kneel and pray.

MIRYAM   Who is that man they call Kepa?

SIMON   You recognise him?

MIRYAM   His presence seems somehow familiar.
As is the other he spoke of. Yeshu.
The name sends shivers through my memory.
You said I must remember this Kepa.
He seems so close, and yet so far away.
Kepa. Yeshu. Yacob—I know him too.
Yes. They followed Yeshu. And so did I!
The crowds, the dust, the days Yeshu sweated
beneath a midday sun, preaching of heaven.
I heard him and loved him; I was there!
And as I loved him, so Yeshu loved me.
The past swallows me: I can scarcely stand.

Anan screams, off. Enter Zebah and other Nazoraeans, carrying Anan.

ZEBAH   Yahweh struck him as he prayed. He is dead.

SAPPHIRA   Kepa, is this what you call Yahweh's judgement?
Murderer! You killed him! You and your thugs!

KEPA   The woman is hysterical. Hold her down.

Sapphira takes out a dagger.

SAPPHIRA   I'll allow you no other opportunity. Sheol awaits
your arrival, Kepa; let our deaths the angel record
against your name.

Sapphira stabs herself.

KEPA   What sad day is this that foul Beelzebub
should thus steal two among our brightest stars.
Yahweh's love is terrible, but must be obeyed.
As Yeshu was bound upon a cross of fire,
so must we accept destiny's burden
and subvert our desires to Yahweh's will.
Let this be our lesson learnt in pain today.
Hold! Who is this? Spies among us! Zebah!

Simon and Miryam step forwards.

SIMON   No need to shout, Kepa. You know me.

KEPA   Simon Magus. We are honoured by your
        presence.

SIMON   Do not lie. I see your heart well enough.
        I have brought you an old friend to visit.

KEPA   Her? You are mistaken. She's unknown to me.

SIMON   Look again. You will see that I am not.

KEPA   Your market trick impressed the ignorant,
        but I know your power's origination,
        as do others in Jerusalem, magician.
        Your safety is far less than you believe.

SIMON   You recognise this woman, then?

KEPA   We have nothing to exchange with this man.
        Let us depart.

YACOB   One moment, Kepa. I recognise her.
        It has been a long time: twenty-one years.
        Yet suffering hasn't changed her from what
        she was; surely you recognise her too.
        Allow me, after all these years, to speak
        your blessed name, Miryam of Magdala.
        Welcome back to holy Jerusalem.
        Kiss me, sister. This is a happy day.

While Yacob talks, Kepa talks on one side to Zebah, who exits.

KEPA   What is your purpose here, Simon Magus?

SIMON   You speak to me as to an enemy.
        Yet you could learn from me if you so choose,
        for he who taught your master also taught me.
        Yeshu and I were desert brothers once,
        two among thirty disciples who lived
        to learn at Yohannes, the baptiser's, feet.
        Our separate wisdom flows from the same source.

KEPA   I remain unimpressed, Simon Magus.
That you and Yeshu were fellow pupils
I cannot accept, your path of evil
being so opposite that of Yeshu.

SIMON   You have not asked me here, so I shall not
teach you the manner of your errors.
But your wait for Yeshu I cannot pass.
A body once dead is dead, and does not rise.
Neither will Yeshu return in the way
you anticipate, nor be useful if he did.
He achieves more out of the body than in.

KEPA   I see neither how you could know this,
nor why you come to speak of it today.

MIRYAM   I know why. It is to my benefit.
My name is Miryam of Magdala,
loved follower of Yeshu, our master,
and I remember you too well, Kepa.
Do you remember me? I think you do.
Nor is this silence untypical of you.
From the beginning, when Yeshu freed my mind
of demons and brought me to the centre
of his wisdom, you resented my presence.
In part this was because I am a woman,
and you think only men worthy to walk
the path of wisdom. But also you hated
the love Yeshu showed to me; he kissed me
differently to the way he kissed you all.
Because I came from Magdala, a city
well known for its brothels and perversions,
you called me whore, and ridiculed my love,
despite the purity of my devotions.
Yacob can witness me in this regard
Yeshu and I would have married, except

the duties of his mission precluded it.
Knowing this, I accepted my destiny
and served Yeshu to my capacity.
Throughout his trials my love was constant,
as was that of all the women with me.
When Yeshu was taken by the Sanhedrin,
presented to judgement, and crucified,
we women could do nothing; but we stood
our ground, we let our weak selves be counted.
Which cannot be said of his disciples.
They scattered on Yeshu's capture, and made
so little effort to support him that
Yoseph of Arimathea, who until
that time had kept his devotion hidden
for fear of the Sanhedrin's reprisals,
was forced to take charge of the burial,
placing Yeshu's body in his family crypt,
thus revealing his secret devotion
to his numbered enemies' derision.
He showed more courage in this, and greater
sense of duty, than Yeshu's chosen twelve.
But none could equal Kepa's hypocrisy.
Three times he was asked by witnesses if
he knew Yeshu: three times he denied he did.
Why? Because he placed his lying carcass
before his own master's integrity.
Any conscience-driven soul would have hung
its head in shame; Kepa raised his, claiming
he was Yeshu's chosen first disciple,
he was the rock upon whom all must stand.
He could never forgive me for being
the first to witness Yeshu's resurrection.
But I was given that honour because

Yeshu loved me more than him, and because
I had the courage to walk past Roman
noses to Yeshu's tomb, where Kepa did not.
Only when I safely returned did he attend.
From then Kepa's jealousy inspired him
to consolidate his dark position.
He began by killing the betrayer,
Judas Iscariot. Rumour suggests
Judas hanged himself, but Kepa has preached
he fell in the field his blood money
bought and burst open, mingling his entrails
with the dust. Do people just burst open?
Or do knives help? I feared then for my life.
Fortunately, Kepa's low estimation
of women deemed me unworthy of death.
Instead, insinuations of whoredom
and my impurity were sufficient
to drive me from Jerusalem's safety,
out into the wilderness, and beyond.
Lone women have hard passage through this world
when their community spurns them, and kept
from the source from which we renew ourselves,
all strives to shut out soul from spirit,
and encompasses it with fleshly concerns.
At length doubt assailed me, that I imagined
Yeshu's love, his resurrected spirit;
then, by degrees, I forgot what I am.
Eventually, Kepa's mouthings came true,
and I ended in the brothels of Tyre,
yet another soul lost in darkness.
That I now know myself more than ever
I did I owe to the efforts of Simon,
and to this meeting here, Kepa, with you.

For this you have my gratitude. Shalom,
brother. May peace one day abide with you.

KEPA Your brothel years have fed you diseases
which eat your brain, and turn your thoughts to
dung.

MIRYAM Allow me to disabuse you of one
further misconception. You say your name
of 'Kepa' was given you by Yeshu
because you are the rock upon whose strength
his future teaching must rest. This is false.
Yeshu named you Kepa because he saw
your heart's hardness, its total lack of love.
As in much of Yeshu's words, you misunderstood.

KEPA Who believes this magician and his whore?
You see, all here know you produce these slanders
only to steal their living souls, and reduce
their purity to perversion and death.
Look, magician, at what we think of you.
We laugh. Brothers, sisters, laugh with me.
I laugh at words empty both of truth and threat.

Exeunt Nazoraeans, in silence. They quickly return, followed by Roman soldiers. Enter Zebah and centurion.

ZEBAH This is the magician.

CENTURION Take him.

KEPA Now Simon, we see who is the magus here.

Exeunt.

♋   ♋   ♋

Enter Hebron with Joel and Adina.

JOEL Our families won't be hurt, will they?

ADINA They're nothing to any of this. They're faithful.

[99]

JOEL   And us. We're faithful too.

ADINA   We've been purified.

JOEL   In the Temple.

ADINA   Weeks ago.

JOEL   Months.

ADINA   We're yours.

JOEL   Just keep our families uninvolved.

Enter Ananias. Hebron takes him aside, and they speak. Enter Simon, flying.

ADINA   I'm afraid.

JOEL   With good reason. But we have made our choice. He must follow it now to the end.

ADINA   If I survive today I'm taking my family and leaving Jerusalem tomorrow.

JOEL   You'll be chasing me to the city gates.

ANANIAS   There's nothing to fear, my friends. We have no intention of harming either you or your families. Do you serve Yahweh?

JOEL   Of course.

ADINA   With all our hearts.

ANANIAS   Then we are brothers, and feel towards each other only love. Tell me then you will testify to Simon Magus' magical practices before the appropriate authorities.

ADINA   But you are the authorities.

HEBRON   Rome is in authority here. We serve Judaea only.

ANANIAS   There will be shortly a hearing before King Agrippa and the new procurator, Antonius Felix. The Magus, your former master, is to be arraigned before them.

ADINA   You have him in custody?

HEBRON   That is not your concern.

ANANIAS   Present or not, we want you to repeat before the procurator what you have already made plain to us.

JOEL   And then?

ANANIAS   You are free to go.

HEBRON   With our blessings.

ADINA   And our families?

ANANIAS   Will you testify or not?

JOEL   We will.

Enter Mordecai with Zacharia.

ANANIAS   Good. You will be required shortly. Hebron will accompany you until you are.

ZACHARIA   Joel? Adina? Is that you? No, wait. I want to talk.

Exeunt Hebron, Adina and Joel.

ZACHARIA   What's happening? Why are they here? Where's the Magus? You agreed he wouldn't be touched.

ANANIAS   Our agreement holds until one of us dies. Guards.

Enter two guards.

ZACHARIA   What's this?

MORDECAI   We can't have you walking the streets, free to say who organised the plot against Jonathan.

ZACHARIA   I expected as much for myself. But the Magus? You'll allow him to leave Jerusalem unharmed?

ANANIAS   Take him away.

ZACHARIA   You'll rot in Sheol for this! You're—

The guards strikes Zacharia. Exeunt guards, carrying Zacharia.

ANANIAS   What news of Jonathan?

MORDECAI   As yet unsighted. Either the Romans took him, or some in the crowd.

ANANIAS   How badly wounded was he?

MORDECAI He looked to me to be losing too much blood to live long.

ANANIAS Perhaps his survival is to our greater benefit than his immediate death.

MORDECAI I don't understand.

ANANIAS If Jonathan dies—and according to your witness he must—we can directly blame the magician and his spells. The populace consequently incensed by Jonathan's death, the magician's base of support will be corroded, and we have him.

Enter Hebron. Exit Simon, flying above.

HEBRON The procurator is ready.

ANANIAS Let us see of what stuff this Antonius Felix is made.

Exeunt.

♋ ♋ ♋

Enter Agrippa, Druscilla and attendants.

AGRIPPA What a nightmare! Half Jerusalem watching, and my hair refuses to sit straight.

DRUSCILLA What of my marriage to Felix? Will the Sanhedrin permit it?

AGRIPPA They salivate at the prospect. It's an impossible mess!

DRUSCILLA Brother, you look positively regal. And your speech was sublime. How soon before marriage will be permitted?

AGRIPPA Immediately one small problem is resolved. It seems Felix's foreskin stands between you and their unrestricted approval.

DRUSCILLA Inform them I find it no restriction at all.

ATTENDANT His excellency, procurator Antonius Felix.

Enter Antonius Felix, Marcus, centurion and soldiers. Enter Ananias, Hebron and members of the Sanhedrin. Enter Mordecai, Joel and Adina.

MARCUS The court is now in attendance to hear the accusations made against Simon Magus, the magician from Samaria. Bring in the prisoner.

JOEL This wasn't part of our arrangement.

ADINA We can't withstand the Magus.

JOEL Not face to face.

ADINA We're just bugs to him.

JOEL If he sees us here, we're dead.

ADINA You've got to take us away from.

JOEL At once. Before he comes.

FELIX Who are these?

ANANIAS The witnesses against Simon Magus. They're terrified the magician will kill them by magic if he finds them present.

FELIX Let's test this magician's power. Keep them here but hide them, so neither he nor the court may observe their presence.

Joel and Adina are hidden. Enter Simon Magus and centurion. The soldiers draw ranks behind Simon.

FELIX Welcome, Magus. Relax, please: you're our guest.
Since my arrival in Jerusalem
no talk but admiration of your powers
has besieged my hearing; it excites me
that today my eyes also were honoured
to feed on evidences of your skill.
An impressive exhibition. In neither Rome
nor its innegligable satellites
have I witnessed a dead man raised to life.

I congratulate you: as do we all.

Our acclamation does not amuse you?

SIMON You acclaim what you did not see.

FELIX You suggest, then, the dead man was not raised?

SIMON Death does not exist, only a translation

from one state of being into the next.

FELIX So if I ordered you executed now,

you could translate yourself back from the dead?

SIMON You think this worth returning to?

FELIX But you could do it?

SIMON Would you recognise me if I did?

FELIX You must back your own powers, magician,

to dare destruction by speaking so.

SIMON Not at all. But I understand that Rome's

legacy of honour rewards obedience.

Now I am here, I expect no less from you.

FELIX This comes as most unanticipated.

First you fly my ordered detention, and then,

when finally you are captured, you turn

and demand recompense for your presence.

Who treats whom with contempt, Simon Magus?

Yet to show Rome's legacy of honour,

as you so term it, I shall not reward you

with what you deserve, but rather with that

which your self-inflated desire demands.

So tell us, how would you be rewarded?

SIMON By having returned to me that which is mine.

FELIX Yes? And what of yours do we possess?

SIMON Come, excellency; enough of these games.

The two Ananias bought to denounce me

are no longer required performers.

The prey being here, dispense with the bait.

FELIX You would sacrifice yourself to save them?

Two whimpering cowards who would betray
their master merely to preserve their skins?
If you want them, Magus, tell us where they are.
Do so, and they are free; fail, and they die.

SIMON   Joel, Adina; come out.

Joel and Adina obey.

FELIX   Your reputation revives.

SIMON   Be ashamed, brothers. Now go.

Exeunt Joel and Adina.

FELIX   Most touching. Yet I remain unconvinced
that your powers match your reputation.
Some test is required, whereby we may judge
more fairly the resources you possess.

ANANIAS   With respect, the man is not to be toyed with.
We have word Jonathan's killer numbers
amongst the magician's closest followers.
Kill him, and wash your hands of the matter.

FELIX   I'm pleased you should say that, Ananias.
For I have word of who gave the assassin
his dagger, and pointed him out the game.

DRUSCILLA   May I make a suggestion?

FELIX   By all means, my darling.

DRUSCILLA   The magician's reputation says he flies.
Let that be the test to prove his powers.

FELIX   Excellent! Magus, do you accept?
Fly tomorrow, and we both acknowledge
your powers, and break free your shackles.
Fail, and we loosen only your soul.

SIMON   Excellency, I freely acknowledge
your absolute power over my body.

FELIX   But will you fly?

SIMON   I shall do what my power allows.

FELIX   Tomorrow at noon in the square, Marcus,
have the adoring populace assembled.
They shall see him shown for the husk he is.
The occasion also shall function
publicly to announce my betrothal
to Druscilla, Judaea's gorgeous star.
What objections you own, Ananias,
you have time to resolve before then.
For the present keep the Magus bonded
his one excellent power is that of escape.
Until then, all depart.

Exeunt.

♋   ♋   ♋

Discover Zacharia, bound.

ZACHARIA   Magus, can you hear me? I'm exhausted.
What I hoped to achieve on your behalf
has proved itself entirely empty.

Enter Simon, flying.

ZACHARIA   Human freedom, you said, consists of but
the right we possess to exercise choice.
In nothing else are we free, but in choice.
You are wrong.
You forgot some manic perversity
rules this world, in whose image we are made,
and thus when given occasion to choose
monsters, not angels, rise from the human will,
diverting what good may chance from altruism
into the callous cauldron of expedience
and self-interested politicking.
Thus choice deports us to a moral hell,
the which we occupy thinking to exert

free will, and good, yet end in corruption,
vomiting vitriol, while humanity's
conscience boils in its own vile juices.
If you can hear me, Magus, know I acted
only in service of the ideal you are.
For whatever evil resulted, forgive me.
My remaining sins I justly carry to the grave.

Enter Ananias, Kepa, Mordecai and executioner.

ANANIAS   No, I am not inclined to hear you.
Your time for acting has come and gone;
the matter resides now in our power.
Mordecai, give that slave his due reward.

*Mordecai signals. The executioner approaches Zacharia, drags him to
one side, and strangles him. Enter Hebron.*

KEPA   My point is that our purposes are one.
Our contribution to Temple maintenance
I shall continue to provide, as agreed.
For the rest, I delivered the magician,
as we all desired, to Roman care.
Surely, this in itself allows me freedom
to share in whatever end Simon shall have.
Allow me that, and all other claims I leave.

ANANIAS   I have no time for this prattle, Kepa.
Forget the Samaritan magician.
Rome means to terminate his messianic
expectations: the matter is at its end.
Mordecai, take his offering. Yes, Hebron?

Zacharia dies, is carried off by the executioner. Exit Simon, flying.

HEBRON   Word is that Rome has Jonathan.
ANANIAS   Alive? He surely must be dead by now:
a hero's blood beats no thicker than ours.
What, still here?

Ananias walks to where Zacharia was strangled.

      KEPA   I desire only that our causes—
  ANANIAS   My desire is that you should leave at once.

Anaias slips.

  ANANIAS   Slaves die no cleaner than they lived.
                Wash away this filth: some unsuspicious
                counsellor walking this way may break his neck.
                This marriage proposal has yet to be discussed.
                Mordecai, call the council.
                If Druscilla's marriage is to occur,
                it might be as well with Yahweh's approval.

Exeunt severally.

♋   ♋   ♋

A bell rings, off. Enter Mordecai and executioner with Zacharia's corpse. A troop of marching soldiers heard, off. Mordecai and the executioner dump the corpse, exeunt. The bell rings, closer.

      LEPER   (*Off*) Unclean! Unclean!

Enter leper.

      LEPER   Unclean!

He approaches the corpse, goes through its clothing. A bird cry, off. Thunder cracks. Enter Endor and two beggars. They approach the leper. The leper moves away.

      LEPER   Unclean! Unclean!

Exit leper. Endor and the beggars approach the corpse. Under Endor's guidance they each take a leg.

    ENDOR   Yes, this is the one. Heave away. For your
              troubles I'll fill your bellies with wine. This way;
              this way.

Exeunt, dragging corpse.

♋ ♋ ♋

Enter Miryam and Thomas. They kneel and pray.

MIRYAM   Immortal Fire, kindle in our souls the good,
whether we ask it of you or not.
But command to leave us everything evil,
though ignorantly we beg it of you.
By your will. Amen, Amen, Amen-Ra.

Miryam and Thomas remain kneeling, continue to pray in silence. Thunder. Bird cries, off. Zacharia's corpse is revealed bound to a pole. Endor appears, above. Lightning. Enter five birds, which swoop on Zacharia. Enter Simon Magus.

ENDOR   Welcome, Magus, to my domain.
In your realm your will's indominable,
but you'll find other forces here hold sway;
and they are not so easily vanquished,
nor will I be as casually cast aside.

Endor motions. Lightning. Zacharia starts screaming. Simon approaches Zacharia. Endor motions again. The birds fly towards Simon. He motions. The birds each burst into flame. Simon motions above Zacharia's head. Zacharia stops screaming. Light, above. The thunder dies. The light intensifies. A light glows inside Zacharia. The light pulls out of him, rises above, disappears. Zacharia's body slumps. The light above fades. Exit Simon Magus.

ENDOR   Belial!

A roar sounds, off. Zacharia's corpse disappears. Exit Endor.

THOMAS   Did you feel a disturbance?
MIRYAM   Some thoughts of Zacharia.
THOMAS   I gained the impression he is dead.
MIRYAM   May his spirit find peace.

THOMAS   Dawn approaches. In only a few hours the Magus
will require us. I think we should withdraw and
sleep a little, that we may be adequately prepared.

MIRYAM   I feel too tired to sleep. But I'll gladly sit with
you.

THOMAS   Lean on me, sister.

MIRYAM   Thank you, brother. Lead the way.

Exeunt.

♋   ♋   ♋

Music. Enter musicians, jugglers, acrobats, followed by a crowd of Jerusalem's citizens. Enter Kepa and Zebah.

ZEBAH   This appears the best position. From here you
will oversee both the Roman position, and the
antics of Simon Magus.

KEPA   When do they come?

ZEBAH   King Agrippa has left his palace. He arrives
shortly. What else do you require?

KEPA   Nothing. All now is in the will of Yahweh and
the power he grants my prayers to defeat Simon
Magus. The magician must not fly today.

ZEBAH   His powers seem considerable.

KEPA   What mortal can withstand the power of the
world's creator? Besides, his power is wholly evil,
while ours is wholly good. No, Zebah, this day
will prove to Jerusalem the strength Yahweh has
granted us Nazoraeans through Yeshu. Wish me
well, and praise the Lord. Now go. The little time
I have left I require to prepare myself.

Exit Zebah. Enter Antonius Felix and Druscilla, Agrippa, Lysias, Marcus, Ananias, Hebron, centurion, Simon Magus and soldiers. Mordecai enters into the crowd.

LYSIAS   Jerusalem, welcome Antonius Felix, Caesar's
representative in Judaea.

The crowd is silent.

AGRIPPA   Come now, Jerusalem. What way is this to
venerate Rome's lawful extension?

The crowd hisses.

ANANIAS   Know Yahweh today has approved the marriage
of Druscilla, our noble King's sister, to Felix, our
noble ruler from Rome.

LYSIAS   Judaea, welcome your benefactor, procurator
Antonius Felix!

The crowd falls silent.

FELIX   Jerusalem, I stand here a humbled man.
Your loving acceptance of my presence
and my betrothal today to Druscilla,
King Agrippa's most beautiful sister,
suggests an harmonious relationship
between our too-long contending peoples.
On many issues Judaea and Rome
previously have stood opposed, but one thought
today unites us: our mutual desire for peace.
That desire I whole-heartedly support,
and who think so too have nothing to fear
from me or my military legions.
But let us forget these trifles: you here
today are peaceful citizens, and free,
and your loyalty deserves a reward.
For your amusement, then, and to garland
our joyful betrothal, Simon Magus,
the proclaimed magician, will this afternoon
demonstrate the full power of his magic.
Magus, join us in the popular eye.

For our collective witnessing, and to show
he is no charlatan, the Magus will fly.
Succeed, and he's free; fail, and he dies.
Magus, the day is now entirely yours.
Our breath is bated. Spread your wings and soar!

SIMON   Thank you, Jerusalem, for this opportunity
to show you the extent of my powers.
I must begin, however, with a confession.
For the truth is, despite my reputation,
I myself possess no magical skills at all.
It is true. I am empty of magic.
You may ask on what, then, my reputation rests,
and I would have to acknowledge, on a lie.
Whatever happens works itself through me,
occurring wholly without my conscious will.
Any strength I have consists in but one skill,
that I can remove myself from myself
and allow to flow what the powers choose.
Silence! I am invited, so will have my say.
That power, compared to which we are nothing,
flows not only through me, but through you all,
through, in fact, the whole manifest world.
As a power it is intangible, because
so subtle and all-transcending, yet by
our lesser awareness it can, in part, be known.
To show you the nature of that power,
if in a much reflected and diminished form,
I have been placed today before you all;
thus, by the will of those I most obey,
its secret nature I will now reveal.
Behold, Jerusalem, that spiritual force
which your primitive rituals ignore
the manifest extension of the hidden Fire!

Simon motions. Flames leap up all over the stage. The crowd screams.
Simon motions again. The flames die away.

FELIX   We are impressed.
          But we do not, as yet, see you flying.

SIMON   Your senses are confused. I am now flying,
          and ever have been flying since I arrived.

FELIX   Is that so? Where? Your feet are on the earth.

SIMON   My feet indeed are earthed, yet still I fly.

KEPA   Jerusalem, the Magus cannot fly
          because Yahweh's power inhibits it.
          In all that is, is the strength of Yahweh
          the good, the peaceful, they are Yahweh's gift,
          which we, Judaea's chosen—
          People! Listen! I speak the truth you need.
          None but Yahweh Sabaoth can guide us:
          only Yahweh and his illumined prophets,
          proved so by scriptural signs and miracles.
          Jerusalem! The Magus is not of these.
          His prostration to the twinned evils of
          magic and self-inflation is blasphemy
          which condemns not only him, but all those—
          Judaea, listen! I speak but to your good!

Thunder. An eclipse of the sun begins.

CROWD   The sun!—What's happening?—The sun is being
          eaten!—It's the magician!—The magician bewitches
          the sky!

Thomas and Miryam come out of the crowd, stand by Simon.

MIRYAM   This is an eclipse only, nothing more.
          You have nothing to fear of the Magus:
          neither his power manifests evil,
          nor does his will work but for your inner good.

THOMAS   Procurator, Rome's policies abhor revolt.
Bring down your soldiers and preserve us,
before this meeting ends in violence.
FELIX   Marcus, withdraw your men.

The centurion signals; the soldiers draw back. The stage becomes darker.

CROWD   The magician's power eats the sun!—Kill him!—
Kill them all!

Citizen 8 steps out of the crowd.

CITIZEN 8   Magus, you helped me when I was needy;
I return to you now the service I owe.
Jerusalem, I am he whose sick daughter
two days ago the Magus snatched from death.
I know to say it may seem blasphemy,
and even I doubted I owned the strength to speak,
but the magician's power has no evil;
it is directed only to our good.
My wondrous experience confirms it:
but for the Magus my daughter would have died.

More thunder. Lightning. Enter five birds, crying.

CROWD   Blasphemy!—The magician's power is evil!—He
would bewitch us!—Kill the blasphemer!—Tear
out his tongue!

The crowd attacks Citizen 8. His daughter runs out of the crowd to him. Enter Mordecai and two assistants, carrying Jonathan's corpse.

GIRL   Daddy! Daddy!
CROWD   She's the girl!—She's full of daemons! Stop her
before she kills us too!—Kill them both!

The crowd attacks the girl. Her father is killed, then she is, too.

MORDECAI   Jonathan is dead!
ANANIAS   Never! Not when tongue exists to praise him.

Jerusalem! Here lies my dear brother.
Dead through Beelzebub's malevolent magic.
Dead by the magician's murderous will!

Lightning. The eclipse is at its fullest. Enter Endor.

CROWD   The magician's daemon!—Save us!—Kill him!—
Kill the magician!—Kill them all!

SIMON   Step behind me.

CROWD   Kill them! Kill them! Kill them! Kill them!

Thomas and Miryam stand behind Simon. The chanting crowd surrounds them.

SIMON   My power, why have you forsaken me?

The crowd pauses, continuing to chant. Then the crowd steps in and kills them. As Simon Magus disappears beneath the crowd lights appear above. Music. Exit Endor. The lights intensify, filling the stage. Simon Magus lifts into the air, accompanied by Thomas and Miryam, one on either side. The three hover in the air. Their bodies lie on the stage. Exeunt all but the three. Simon Magus, Miryam and Thomas exeunt above. The light fades. Music ends.

Background Notes

SIMON MAGUS, HERETIC

We know very little about the first century Gnostic teacher Simon Magus, and even that little is only recorded by his enemies. To them Simon Magus was 'the father of all heresies'. As the Church Fathers Epipanius and Iraneaus declared:

> From the time of Christ to our own day the first
> heresy was that of Simon the magician. ... All those
> who in any way corrupt the truth, and harm the
> teaching of the Church, are the disciples or succes-
> sors of Simon Magus of Samaria.[1]

However in this, as in much else about the Gnostics, the Christian Fathers were wrong. Simon Magus was the originator of neither Gnosticism nor of Christian heresy. Numerous Christian Gnostic groups were active from the late first century. Their roots are visible in the teachings of the Pythagoreans, Orphics and Zoroastrian Magi. Gnostic ideas are complemented by the mystic schools of the Egyptian Hermeticists, Neo-Platonists and Theurapeutai, and the esoteric schools of Persia. Spiritually and intellectually, Simon Magus trod a mystic path that had numerous contemporary branches, whose doctrines had been developing around the Mediterranean for at least five hundred years.

This diversity of doctrines means the designation of Simon Magus as the first Christian heretic cannot derive from the unorthodoxy of his teaching, especially given that during his lifetime there was no orthodox Christian doctrine from which it could diverge. The process of generating orthodoxy began late in the second century, when the first Church Fathers began condemning those they didn't want in their Church. Calling Gnostic Christians heretics, and naming Simon Magus their father, provided one of the foundational myths on which Christian doctrine was built over the second to sixth centuries. During that period, as Christianity grew from a small movement in Jerusalem to the state religion of Rome, Christian leaders ordered that all so-called heretical texts be burned. With Gnostic texts destroyed, no one was able to evaluate the veracity of Fathers' claims.

This situation changed in 1773, with the discovery of a papyrus codex written in Coptic (Egyptian Greek) that contained a fourth century Gnostic book, *Pistis Sophia*. Another Coptic codex was discovered in 1896 that preserved three more Gnostic texts: *The Gospel of Mary, Apocryphon of John*, and *The Sophia of Jesus Christ*. These allowed scholars to begin the task of matching the Gnostic originals against the Fathers' representations of Gnostic thought. They discovered that the Fathers had either misread the texts, had not understood them, or had misrepresented them. Scholars' work progressed exponentially when thirteen more Coptic codexes, containing dozens of Gnostic books, were discovered in 1945 near the village of Nag Hammadhi, Egypt. Collectively, these texts showed that Gnostic thought was far more complex, varied and sophisticated than the Fathers' (mis)representations allowed.

GNOSTICISM AND ORTHODOX CHRISTIANITY

During the first two centuries of the common era, Christian Gnostics existed in numerous groups, many viewed themselves as part of a Christian world that extended across the Mediterranean and included Gaul (France), Italy, Cathage (in Libya), Egypt, Lebanon, Syria and Anatolia (Turkey). When the Egyptian Gnostic teacher Valentinus travelled from Alexandria to Rome around 140 CE., he was so much part of the Church that he was nominated to the position of bishop. Yet when the Church Father Tertullian wrote fifty years later, he identified the Valentinians as heretics. He wanted to establish an authoritative Christian theology, and did not see a place for Gnostic teaching in it.[2]

A century earlier, the first churches had no single set of doctrines. *The Acts of the Apostles* and Paul's letters repeatedly record Paul contending with schisms and alternative gospels:

> Any newcomer has only to proclaim a new Jesus, different from the one we preached ... and you welcome him with open arms. (*2 Corinthians* 11 4)
> ... It is clear there are serious differences among you. What I mean are all these slogans that you have, like 'I am for Paul', 'I am for Apollos', 'I am for Cephas', 'I am for Christ'. (*1 Corinthians* 1 11-12)
> ... I am astonished at the promptness with which you have turned away from the one who called you and have decided to follow a different version of the Good News. .... Let me warn you that if anyone preaches a version of the Good News different from the one we have already preached to you, whether it be ourselves or an angel from heaven, he is to be condemned. (*Galatians* 1 6-8)[3]

The final quote from *Galatians* set the stance the Fathers adopted: intolerance of divergent thinking. In the latter half of the second century, as the Fathers began establishing a uniform doctrine and a centralised ecclesiastical authority, the

Gnostics proved resistant. Some claimed they possessed a gnosis, a secret spiritual knowledge, which made guidance from the Church's clerical hierarchy unnecessary. This knowledge comes from within the individual, through direct insight. Furthermore, they claimed this knowledge was taught by Jesus:

> Jesus said, If those who lead you say to you, 'See, the kingdom is in heaven', then the birds of the heaven will precede you. If they say to you, 'It is in the sea', then the fish will precede you. But the kingdom is within you and it is without you. If you will know yourselves, then you will be known and you will know that you are the sons of the Living Father. But if you do not know yourselves, then you are in poverty and you are poverty.[4]

This is from *The Gospel of Thomas*, an early Gnostic work that consists of Jesus' sayings. Some of *Thomas's* sayings are echoed in *Mathew*, *Mark* and *Luke*, which has led to the theory that *Thomas* may not only predate the writing of the New Testament gospels, but that it may be a legitimate source for what Jesus actually said. This continues to be debated by early Christian scholars.

What we can be sure of is that the above saying encapsulates the Gnostic view that there is no need for intermediaries between a worshipper and the Living Father, because each seeker already possesses the kingdom within. This interior view of spirituality was rejected by the Fathers. In *John* Jesus states, 'No one shall come to the Father except through Me' (14:6). The apostles were Jesus' representatives on Earth after he died, so the Fathers sought to establish apostolic authority through Simon Peter. In doing so, they rejected the Gnostic emphasis on each worshipper's inwardness. The Gnostics pushed back, and tensions grew:

After we [Gnostics] went forth from our home, and came into this world, and came into being in the world of bodies, we were hated and persecuted, not only by those who are ignorant, but also by those who think that they are advancing the name of Christ, since they were unknowingly empty, not knowing who they are, like dumb animals.[5]

The Fathers viewed this as a challenge to their authority. Such was Irenaeus' outrage at Gnostic arrogance that he wrote:

They consider themselves 'mature', so that no-one can be compared to them in the greatness of their gnosis, not even if you mention Peter or Paul or any of the other apostles. ... They imagine they have discovered more than the apostles. ... If anyone yields himself to them like little sheep, and follows out their practice and their redemption, such a person becomes so puffed up that ... he walks with a strutting gait and a supercilious countenance, possessing all the pompous air of a cock![6]

The Fathers replied to this challenge by declaring Gnostics heretics and set about suppressing them. The task took until the sixth century, but by anathematising non-orthodox congregations and burning their books, they succeeded. Gnostic thought and feeling was banished from Christianity, Gnostic groups disappeared from public view, and the extensive literature they produced was almost completely destroyed.

GNOSTIC PHILOSOPHY

As a movement, Gnosticism was concerned with investigating spiritual realities, not with establishing a worldly regime. This is arguably a major reason Christianity survived and Gnosticism did not. In the words of Monoimus, an Arabian contemporary of Valentinus, the purpose of the gnostic search is to:

> Cease to seek after God [as without you], and the universe, and things similar to these; seek Him out of yourself, and say, 'My god, my mind, my reason, my soul, my body.' And learn where sorrow and joy comes from, and love and hate, and waking though one would not, and sleeping though one would not, and getting angry though one would not, and falling in love though one would not. And if you should closely investigate these things, you will find Him in yourself, one and many, just as the atom; thus finding from yourself a way out of yourself[7]

Gnostic teachings were not unfirm. Many Gnostic writings offer poetic responses to spiritual quandaries rather than fixed doctrines. The variety of their ideas may also be explained, at least in part, by Gnostic schools and congregations incorporating the cultural, religious and ritualistic traditions that existed within their local communities. Thus while Christian Gnostic schools were the most numerous, there were also Egyptian, Jewish, Zoroastrian and Arabic Gnostics. With no 'command centre', each group was free to formulate its teaching in its own manner. Most did so, and recorded their thoughts in writing. This resulted in an extensive literature, full of fascinating insights and speculations. This literature became so vast that Irenaeus complained:

> Every one of them generates something new every day, according to his abilities; for no one is considered initiated [or 'mature'] amongst them unless he develops some enormous fictions![8]

Despite the divergences, a number of core ideas underlie Gnostic thought. Chief amongst these is the Sophia myth. To the Gnostics, that from which everything derives, to which we nominally give the name God, is unfathomable, both unknown and unknowable. Different schools variously named the unknowable unknown the Boundless Power, the Perfect Aeon, the Universal Root, the Abyss, Silence, and Father Over All.

After a timeless period the Boundless Power emanated a syzygy (linked pair) of powers, Nous (Mind) and Ennoea (Thought). Nous is a male power, Ennoea female. After another period, Ennoea emanated a series of Aeons, twelve in number, each containing its own syzygy. A last Aeon, Sophia (Wisdom) was also emanated. Sophia was female and had no syzygy partner. She was also known as the Thirteenth Aeon. Together these thirteen constituted the Pleroma, an entirely spiritual realm, variously called 'the fullness of perfection' and 'the godhead'.

After yet another period Sophia decided that she wanted to create in the same manner as Ennoea had done, and so gave birth to her own emanation. But because she lacked a syzygy partner her emanation remained formless matter, rude and chaotic. This was named 'the abortion' because it existed outside the perfection of the Pleroma. The chaotic 'abortion' is the material universe.

A ruefully ironic humour animates those who called our world 'the abortion'. Like today, Mediterranean states had pockets of great sophistication and wealth, whose riches depended on enslaved workers. Even among those who were not slaves, social and economic inequality was prevalent. The life experience of common people is reflected in a hymn composed by a Manichean in the second century. It is spoken by a distressed soul surrounded by those who contradictorily subjugate and worship it, from whom it seeks salvation:

You buy me like slaves from thieves,
and you fear and implore me as you do lords.
Like disciples from the world you elect me to be
among the righteous,
and you show me reverence as you do masters.
You smite and hurt me like enemies,
and you save and vivify me like friends.
However, my Fathers, the Light Gods, have power
and might ... .[9]

This hymn embodies the same yearning that orthodox Christianity appealed to: escape from the dark harshness of the world into a post-life paradisaical state. Being a poetical hymn, this deep desire is conjured in general terms. Other Gnostic texts go into considerable detail regarding the material and spiritual domains, the nature of the powers that preside over 'the abortion', and how escape may be achieved.

The material universe is ruled by a number of sovereignties and powers. Our world's ruler is the creator god. In a clear rejection of the god of Judaism and Christianity, Gnostics called this god 'creator' not because he created the world, but because he thought he did. In fact, he was ignorant of the Aeons above him, and that he himself was generated by Sophia. Judaic Gnostics identified the creator god with Yahweh, Valentinius with the demiurge of Plato's *Timaeas*.

However, in manifesting herself down to this level Sophia found herself detained by these lesser powers, and she soon forgot who she was, that she came from above, and that the world was not her home. Seeing this, and filled with compassion at her plight, the Boundless Power manifested another Aeon, the Logos, also called the Christ, which it sent down to awaken Sophia from her sleep in the body, and to help her escape the rule of the ignorant creator god. Ascending out of the physical world with the help of the Logos, Sophia overcame the rulers of each Aeon in turn, until she returned to the origin and found her rest in Silence, reunited with that from which she originally came.

Sophia, in this lowest world, the Gnostics identified with the individual human spirit. Thus each human being's task is to respond to the call of the Logos and return to its source.

THE CHRISTIAN GNOSIS

The contribution Gnosticism made to the evolution of orthodox Christianity has never been adequately acknowledged by orthodox apologists. Yet it was considerable. The Fathers began formulating their own creeds in refutation of Gnostic writings. Two key Gnostic contributors to this process were the Alexandrian teacher, Basilides (c. 120 CE.), who was well versed in the Hebrew scriptures, quoted from the Pauline letters, and wrote at least twenty-four books of commentaries on early Christian texts, and Marcion (c. 150 CE.), who was the first to draw up a canon of New Testament books—although in his endeavour to free Christianity from Judaic doctrines, he excluded the four gospels and many Pauline letters. That Gnostic conceptions should have left their imprint on orthodox teachings is thus to be expected. The prologue of *The Gospel According to John* is an obvious example: the identification of the Saviour both with Light and with the Logos of the Sophia-myth is entirely consistent with Gnostic teaching.

To all Christians Jesus was the saviour, the redeemer. But there was a great deal of variation in conceptions of his nature. To the first century Docetists, Jesus was not flesh and blood; he was an entirely spiritual being who appeared on Earth and taught in a spectral body only. For the second century Adoptionists, Jesus was a man into whom the Christ spirit entered at baptism. This is also the conception of Jesus presented by *Mark*, which starts at the baptism for the same reason: only with the entrance of the Spirit did Jesus become the Christ—or Chrestos. (The difference is that 'Christ' is the anointed Messiah of Judaism, whereas 'Chrestos' means the good, and was used to designate a wise, spiritually elevated person. For this reason Marcion referred to 'Jesus, the Chrestos', rejecting the designation Jesus, the Christ.) To other Gnostics Jesus became the Christ (or Chrestos) only after his resurrection, which was spiritual, not fleshly. But to all Gnostics Jesus and Christ were two separate entities. And if the Christ spirit could enter Jesus, so it could enter into anyone who practised Gnostic teaching:

> Jesus said: Whoever drinks from my mouth will become as I am. I myself shall become he, and things hidden shall be revealed to him.[10]

HISTORICAL SOURCES

The three sources of information on Simon Magus are: (1) *The Acts of the Apostles*, (2) the writings of the Church Fathers, and (3) legendary material from the Clementine literature. These sources share an extreme antagonism towards the Magus. Their preference for polemic over fact means the reader must sift the material to separate possible history and philosophy from exaggeration, deliberate misrepresentation and, in places, ludicrous invention.

An indication of the difficulties involved becomes apparent when we examine the earliest reference to Simon Magus. This is in the writings of the Church Father Justin Martyr (c. 150 CE.). He wrote to his Roman followers of a certain Samaritan, Simon:

Who in the reign of Claudius Caesar [41-45 CE.] wrought many magic wonders by the art of the demons who possessed him, and as a god was honoured with a statue by you, which statue was erected in the river Tiber, between the two bridges, with the following inscription: Simoni Deo Sancto [To Simon, the Holy Roman God].[11]

Two problems immediately surface. The first is that Justin was writing almost one hundred years after the chief activity of Simon Magus, yet provides the earliest historical evidence. The second is that in 1574 a large marble fragment was found in the island of Tiber bearing the inscription, 'Semoni Sanco Deo Fidio'. Clearly this was Justin's source; equally clearly, it was dedicated to a Sabine god, Fidio, and not to Simon at all. What Justin offered as historical evidence was shown to be misinterpretation. Unfortunately, procedural negligence is not unique to Justin, but is common to all the Fathers. It is further compounded by the tendency of the later Fathers to take as fact the often suppositional testimony of earlier writers.

Irenaeus (c. 190 CE.) is the second to write of Simon Magus, and the first to mention Simon's association with a prostitute, Helen. He is followed by Tertullian (c. 199 CE.), who copies Irenaeus's account. Then comes Hippolytus (c. 210 CE.), the only Father to quote directly from writings attributed to Simon Magus. The remaining Fathers who wrote of Simon are Origenes (c. 240 CE.), Philastrius (died 387 CE.), Epiphanius (died 404 CE.), and Theodoretus (died c. 453 CE.). All referred to Simon only in works dealing with heretics and heresies. The one remaining source, the Clementine literature, dates from the beginning of the third century. But the lateness of them all, coupled to their polemical nature, constitutes a body of material that offers no certainty of historical accuracy.

Historically, the major difficulty in trying to understand Gnostic thought was that before the discovery of Coptic codexes the only records of Gnostic doctrines were the writings of the Church Fathers. Their untrustworthiness was revealed when *The Gospel of Mary* was discovered in 1896, a text from which Irenaeus made extensive extracts. After reviewing both sets of writings, A.V. Harnack observed:

> We are thus for the first time in a position to control by the original the presentation of the Gnostic System as rendered by the Church Father. The result of the examination shows, as we might have expected, that owing to omissions, and because no effort was made to understand his opponents, the sense of the by no means absurd speculations of the Gnostics has been ruined by the Church Father.[12]

SIMON MAGUS' BIOGRAPHY

Gleaning what we can from the above three sources, Simon Magus was likely born in Samaria, in the village of Gitta. Nothing more is known of him until he became a disciple of John the Baptist. When the Baptist was killed Simon was in Alexandria, learning magic.

What exactly is meant by 'magic' remains unclear. *The Gospel of Mark* depicts Jesus as a magician, walking on water, miraculously curing the sick and troubled, changing water into wine, and bringing the dead back to life. Possessing magical powers appears to have been a requirement for first century sages. Apollonius of Tyana was similarly described as possessing psychic abilities that enabled him to foresee future events, peer into the past, and read people's hearts. Like Jesus, he healed the sick and cured diseased minds. While he was held in high esteem for centuries as a virtuous and wise Pythagorean philosopher, once he was incorporated into later Christian polemical writing he, like Simon Magus, was condemned for being in thrall to demons.[13]

With respect to Simon Magus and magical practices, it is significant that the Magus studied magic in Alexandria. At that time the city was a key trading centre. As a result it was hugely cosmopolitan—an Indian yogi famously visited in the first century—providing a home for numerous schools that taught every kind of philosophy, spirituality and science. It was also a leading centre of Gnostic thought, practice and writing, as well as for Hermeticism, whose teaching included philosophic speculations, mystical experiences and magical practices. I will discuss Hermeticism shortly.

Returning from Egypt, Simon found his fellow disciples had elected Dositheos as head of John the Baptist's followers. The Clementine writings record that Simon accepted the position of deputy, but that Dositheos still feared Simon's presence, so when they were alone together he started beating the Magus with a rod. To his surprise, the rod passed right through Simon's body, which had become smoke. Dositheos immediately fell to his knees and worshipped the Magus.

Simon then went travelling. He preached in public, using magic to impress and convert listeners to his teaching. Neither *The Acts of the Apostles* nor the Church Fathers offer insights into the nature of his magic, nor what deeds he performed, but the Clementine literature gives numerous examples. Simon supposedly could:

> Dig through mountains, pass through rocks ... make a beard grow upon a boy's chin, fly in the air, become gold. .... In his house dishes are brought of themselves to him. He makes spectres appear in the

market place; when he walks out statues move, and shadows go before him which he says are souls of the dead.[14]

The Fathers wrote that Simon's followers practised necromancy, used incantations to summon demons, and were sexually promiscuous. Connected with this latter charge, Simon found a prostitute named Helen in Tyre and bought her freedom. To the Fathers, Simon's interest in her was sexual, but certain philosophic ideas are central to their association. I will consider these in the next section.

According to the Clementine literature, Simon's death occurred in Antioch when, in combat with Peter to decide whose power was greater, and flying with the aid of demons, Peter's prayers caused Simon Magus to fall to his death. The Church Father Hippolytus also records Simon's death, but it is in quite different circumstances:

> And towards the end of his career ... he settled under a plane tree and continued his teaching. And finally running the risk of exposure through the length of his stay, he said that if he were buried alive he would rise again on the third day. And he did actually order a grave to be dug by his disciples and told them to bury him. So they carried out his orders, but he has stopped away until the present day, for he was not the Christ.[15]

Clearly, this is invented to show Simon's inferiority to Jesus, who did successfully rise on the third day.

Collectively, these accounts cannot be considered to constitute a real biography. In fact, take out the unhistorical Clementine material and the transparently propagandising *Acts* story, and all we are left with is that Simon Magus was born in

Gitta, Samaria, studied with John the Baptist, practised some form of magic learned In Egypt during the reign of Claudius Caesar, and was accompanied by a prostitute named Helen. Even this little is largely speculative. Simon is lost in legend, his historical presence no more than a ghostly shimmer.

SIMON MAGUS AND HELEN

Simon's association with Helen was first noted by Irenaeus. He wrote:

> He took round with him a certain Helen, a hired prostitute from the Phoenician city Tyre, after he had purchased her freedom, saying she was the first conception (or Thought) of his Mind, the Mother of All, by whom in the beginning he conceived in his Mind the making of the angels and archangels. That this Thought, leaping forth from him, and knowing what was the will of her Father, descended to the lower regions and generated the Angels and Powers, by whom also he said this world was made. And after she had generated them, she was detained by them through envy, for they did not wish to be thought the progeny of any other. ... and she suffered every kind of indignity at their hands, to prevent her reascending to her Father, even to being imprisoned in the human body and transmigrating into other female bodies, as from one vessel to another. She was also in that Helen, on whose account the Trojan Wars arose. ... So she, transmigrating from body to body, and thereby also continually undergoing indignity, last of all even stood for hire in a broth-

el; and she was the 'lost sheep'. Wherefore also he himself had come, to take her away for the first time, and free her from her bonds, and also to guarantee salvation to men by his 'knowledge'.[16]

This is clearly a form of the Gnostic Sophia myth. What isn't clear is if Helen actually existed, if she did but her story was then overlaid with the Sophia myth, or if Irenaeus interpreted literally an allegorical narrative created for teaching purposes. The Jewish prophets used the image of a prostitute to represent lost Israel. This image was subsequently adopted by Gnostics to describe the soul lost in the sensual creation:

> Wise men of old gave the Soul a feminine name. Indeed she is female in her nature as well. She even has her womb. As long as she was with the Father, she was a virgin and in form androgynous. But when she fell down into a body and came to this life, then she fell into the hands of many robbers. And the wanton creatures passed her from one to another and [...] her. Some made use of her [by force], while others did so by seducing her with a gift. In short, they defiled her and she [...] virginity. And in her body she prostituted herself and gave herself to one and all.[17]

Further to this association, the names 'Simon' and 'Helen' are symbolic. Simon derives from the Semitic name for the sun-god, while Helen is connected with the moon, being a variation on the Greek Selene. This latter connection is confirmed in the Clementine literature, where Helen is also named Luna. During this period, the ancient Phoenician cult of sun and moon deities was still practised in Tyre, which further supports the idea of a symbolic relationship between Simon and Helen, the sun and moon, consistent with the Mind-Thought pairing in Gnostic teaching.

Accordingly, it is possible Irenaeus was mistaken when he interpreted the Simon-Helen story as historical, and that even if the story did have some kind of historical basis, it had undergone considerable Gnostic mythologising long before he came into contact with it.

SIMON'S WRITINGS

The Fathers record the names of three works written by Simon or in his name: *The Four Quarters of the World*, *Refutorii Sermones* and *The Great Announcement*. The texts of the first two are lost in their entirety, but Hippolytus made direct quotations from the third, extracts from which it would be useful to present here to give an idea of the Simonian gnosis:

> This is the writing of the revelation of Voice and Name from Thought, the Great Power, the Boundless. ... To you, therefore, I say what I say, and write what I write. And the writing is this. Of the Universal Aeons there are two shoots, without beginning or end, springing from one root, which is the Power invisible, inapprehensible Silence. Of these shoots one is manifested from above, which is the Great Power, the Universal Mind ordering all things, male, and the other, (is manifested) from below, the Great Thought, female, producing all things. ... This is he who has stood, stands, and will stand, a male-female power like the pre-existing Boundless Power, which had neither beginning nor end, existing in oneness. For it is from this that the Thought in the oneness proceeded and became two. ... Hence they pair with

each other being one, for there is no difference between Power and Thought. From the things above is
discovered Power, and from those below Thought. ...
Thus Mind is in Thought—things inseparable from
one another—which although being one are yet
found as two.[18]

The absence of Christian Gnostic elements from this text
indicates it likely either predates Christian Gnosticism of the
first and second centuries, or was produced in a parallel but independent cultural stream. One possible parallel stream is Hermeticism. Hermetic philosophy uses a similar dualistic concep-
tual framework: God as androgyne, the mind being god-like,
male and female coming into existence only after the creation
of the natural world, human beings possessing a mortal body
and an immortal essence, and the existential human spiritual
choice being between physical death or spiritual immortality.[19]

A further potential link is offered by the earliest Hermetic
writing, which was likely produced in Alexandria in the first
century, when Simon Magus was supposed to have studied
there. Moreover, given that four Hermetic texts were found
among the Nag Hammadi codexes, we can see Hermetic writings resonated with Gnostic readers. Conceptually, the above
extracts also suggest that during his time in Alexandria Simon
absorbed Neoplatonic Greco-Egyptian philosophy along with
Hermetic magical practices.

The focus on pairs additionally suggests a resonance with
Persian dualism, particularly the form it took under the influence of the Zoroastrian religion and its leading exponents, the
Magi. Simon Magus's thought shared a number of concepts
central to Zoroastrianism. These include fire, flying and magic.

SIMON MAGUS'S PHILOSOPHY OF MAGIC

We know from the Fathers that magic was central to Simon's philosophy. Another Gnostic teacher, Menander, indicates what his magic might have included. A Samaritan like Simon, Menander's activities were centered in Antioch, an important commercial and literary hub that linked Rome and Greece in the West to Persia in the East. According to both Justin and Irenaeus, Menander was Simon's disciple and successor. As regards Menander's teaching, G.R.S. Mead summarises:

> He seems to have handed on the general outlines of the Gnosis; especially insisting on the distinction between the God over all and the creative power or powers, the 'forces of nature'. Wisdom, he taught, was to be attained by the practical discipline of transcendental 'magic'; that is to say, the Gnosis was not to be attained by faith alone, but by definite endeavour and conscious striving along the path of cosmological and psychological science. Menander professed to teach a knowledge of the powers of nature, and the way whereby they could be subjected to the human will.[20]

Mead is suggesting Menander's magic consisted of a form of psychospiritual transformation, in which individuals strove to gain control over their natural bodily proclivities. This led to their 'magical' inward transformation. While the practice of controlling external nature—including planetary influences—is present in Hermetic spells from the period, Hermetic philosophic texts make clear that human salvation is achieved not by controlling external natural forces but by gaining control over one's own natural desires. This same focus on interior transformation features in Gnostic literature. So whatever form

Simon Magus' magic took, that it had an interior component must be assumed. I will come back to this.

Menander is also a link between the Gnostic and Zoroastrian traditions. Mead suggests that, contrary to the Fathers' dating, Menander should be placed earlier than Simon, and that we should see him as one of the earliest links between Gnosticism and the Zoroastrian Magian tradition. In Simon's case, this link is obvious. Magus is a Magian title, and, like the Zoroastrian religion, Simon uses fire as a key concept and metaphor, although without suggesting it be used ritualistically. Simon's use of fire appears to be only metaphysical and psychospiritual.

Hippolytus gives us further information on this. Simon symbolised the Great Power, the Universal Root, as Fire. Fire has a two-fold nature: the concealed and the manifest. The manifest part is sensory creation; the concealed, non-sensory spiritual reality. Simon further likened the concealed Fire to a treasure-house, while the manifest Fire is like a great Tree. All the parts of this Tree are burning, and are devoured by flame. But the fruit of the Tree has the possibility of perfecting itself, which results in it not being destroyed by flame, but being placed in the treasure-house, imperishable. This fruit is the human soul, which thus has the possibility of transcending the sensory creation and achieving immortality. This imagery, of the Tree and the treasure-house, is common to Magian teachings. It also provides metaphors for the 'magical' inner process of psychospiritual transformation.

One further connection to Zoroastrianism is significant. The best known symbol of Zoroastrianism is the Faravahar, which depicts a man's torso inside a disc that has feathered wings and a tail. This symbol's origins are pre-Persian, being derived from the ancient Assyrian sun god, Ashur. Imagery dating to the ninth century B.C.E. depicts Ashur inside a winged sun disc. In some versions he holds a bow and is shooting an arrow, suggestive of the sun's rays. Winged solar discs were also depicted in Egypt from the third millennium.

This linked sun and wings imagery is repeated in Simon Magus' fire imagery and his magical flight. In his treatment of Zoroastrian fire imagery, Simon seems to have adopted the Neoplationic practice of philosophising ancient religious and poetic imagery. Considering magical flying the same way, that is, allegorically rather than literally, we may associate it with rising through the lesser powers of the sensory creation. Concealed Fire provides the energetic force that makes magical flying possible, just as kundalini is used by Indian yogis to develop siddhis (personal physical and psychic abilities) and escape reincarnation. Thus the concept of magical flight may be read as a technical term, referring to the process of psychospiritual transformation that enables spiritual seekers to become inwardly elevated.

This leaves us to discuss one final aspect of Simon's philosophy: the false creator god of Judaism, which was also adopted by Christianity. Epiphanius wrote:

Ashur, Assyrian sun god, 9th century BCE

And he [Simon] says that this world was constructed defectively by dominions and principalities of evil. ... And he pretended that the Law was not of God, but of the left-hand Power, and that the prophets were not from the Good God but from this or the other Power. ... And all of them [the Prophets] were from the left-hand Power and outside the Perfection, and everyone that believed in the Old Testament was subject to death.[21]

Identifying the Hebrew prophets with imperfect powers is consistent with the stance adopted by other Gnostic teachers.

Given the extent to which Simon references Zoroastrian and Judaic culture, and the absence of Christian imagery, we may conclude his is a non-Christian gnosis. Rather than being a Christian heretic, Simon simply engaged in a form of spirituality independent of the early Church.

SIMON MAGUS IN THE CLEMENTINE LITERATURE

I will now consider the depiction of Simon in the Clementine literature. Scholars agree this literature is legendary rather than historical. It is likely the stories about Simon were initially produced for propaganda purposes by a group called the Ebionites (literally, 'the poor'), who date from the late first or early second centuries. Judaic in orientation, the Ebionites revered Jesus as a man who became a prophet at his baptism, and whose task was to renew the Judaic Law. He was not the Messiah, but would become so at the Second Coming. The Ebionites revered Peter above the other apostles. They were also vehemently opposed to Paul of Tarsus and his gentilising tendencies, for to them Jesus' teachings were for Jews and not gentiles. The Clementine literature came out of this outlook.

In the Clementine version of Simon Magus's story, Clement arrives in Caesarea in Judaea on the eve of the legendary showdown between the Magus and Peter, the apostle. Clementine is a member of Peter's retinue. The Magus is initially routed, runs off, and is pursued by Peter to Tyre, then through Syria, and eventually to Antioch, where Peter's prayers bring down the flying Magus and cause his death.

This was considered straightforward until a German scholar, F.C. Bauer, suggested that the Clementine writer may have used Simon as a stand-in for Paul of Tarsus.

> The remarkable similarity of the doctrinal points at issue in both the Petro-Simonian and the Petro-Pauline controversies cannot be denied. ... Although, of course, it would not be prudent to take the extreme view that wherever Simon Magus is mentioned, Paul is meant, nevertheless we may not unclearly distinguish this identity in at least one strata of the legend.[22]

The possible Ebionite identification of Simon Magus with Paul becomes even more interesting when we realise that Paul was not only a gentiliser of Christianity, and thus an enemy to the Ebionites, but appears also to have shared central ideas with the Gnostics.

THE PETRO-PAULINE CONTROVERSY

Gospel passages suggest the earliest Christians were followers of a man who aimed to reform the Judaic Law:

> Do not imagine that I have come to abolish the Law or the prophets. I have come not to abolish, but to complete them. (*Matthew* 5 17.)

These first followers were based in Jerusalem after Jesus' death, and were called Nazoraeans (see *Acts* 24:5). A sect calling itself Nazoraean existed well into the fourth century, but in their earliest form they seem to have had much in common doctrinally with the Ebionites, who may have been an out-growth of the original Nazoraean community. Whether or not this is so, both were Jewish followers of Jesus, who they con-sidered to be a human teacher, not a divine being, and whose ministry began at the baptism. For both groups Jesus' teach-ings were consistent with the Torah, were meant for Jews only, and he directed his disciples to teach similarly.

> These twelve Jesus sent out, instructing them as fol-lows: 'Do not turn your steps to pagan territory, and do not enter any Samaritan town; go rather to the lost sheep of the House of Israel.' (*Matthew* 10 5-6)

To this those who followed Peter added the doctrine of the last days and that the moment of Jesus' return as Messiah was near at hand. Again, this Messiah was only for the Jews (see *Matthew* 24 1-44). In the four orthodox gospels, it is in *Mat-thew* that the Passion is set into a framework whereby Jesus' messianic role is justified by references to Judaic texts included in Old Testament. Apparently the Nazoraeans also had their own *Gospel According to Matthew*, but it was not the same as the version we have; it may also have been called *The Gospel of the Hebrews*. We have neither texts.

Paul's vision of a universal Christ is quite different from the Jewish Petrine view:

> He is the image of the unseen God and the first-born of all creation, for in him were created all things in heaven and on earth: everything visible and everything invisible, thrones, dominations,

> sovereignties, powers—all things were created
> through him and for him. Before anything was
> created, he existed, and he holds all things in unity.
> (*Colossians*, 1 15-17)

The Pauline Christ is much closer to the Gnostic Logos myth than to any Jewish national Messiah, and his teaching differs from Petrine theology accordingly. Chief among the doctrinal differences are that Paul stresses his mission to the pagans and gentiles, he ignores the doctrine of a returning Messiah by preaching only of the power of the resurrected Christ, and he writes of the kingdom of God not as a Jewish New Jerusalem but as a kingdom which is wholly spiritual in nature.

> I tell you this, brethren; flesh and blood cannot in-
> herit the kingdom of god, nor does the perishable
> [body] inherit the imperishable. (*1 Corinthians*, 15:50)

In the second century, orthodox Christianity reconciled the Petrine and Pauline views. The *Acts* may be read as written not just to document the early post-crucifixtion era, but to harmonise the Petrine and Pauline views of Jesus. Whichever way we read the New Testament, it is clear that in the first century there was no agreed 'Jesus Christ'. Later texts and ecclesiastical declarations reflect a process of theological evolution, in which Jesus is progressively reimaged by his worshippers over the centuries.

The final aspect of the Petro-Pauline controversy of significance here is the fact that Paul considered himself Christ's apostle not on the basis of knowing Jesus personally (his letters show no knowledge of Jesus as a historical person), but on the basis of his inner experiences:

> I know a man in Christ who, fourteen years ago, was caught up—whether still in the body or out of the body, I do not know; God knows—right into the third heaven. I do know, however, that this person ... was caught up into paradise and heard things which must not and cannot be put into human language. (*Corinthians* 12 2-4) ... The Good News I preached is not a human message that I was given by men, it is something I learnt only through a revelation of Jesus Christ. .... God, who had specially chosen me while I was still in my mother's womb, called me through his grace and chose to reveal his Son in me. (*Galatians* 1 11-12,15-16) ... I have been crucified with Christ, and I live now not with my own life but with the life of Christ who lives in me. (*Galatians* 2 19-20)

A side note: The word 'Christ' in Paul's letters may have originally have been 'Chrestos'. Both are Greek words, the first referring to one who is anointed (rubbed with oils to prepare for worship), the second to a person who is good and wise. Tertullian records the earliest Christians called Jesus Chrestos, which suggests 'Chrestos' was later replaced by 'Christ'.

A key point in the above is that Paul, like the Gnostics, emphasised inner experience. The Chrestos is good and wise due to inner qualities. In contrast, the Fathers taught that ecclesiastical authority primarily derives not from inner qualities, but was vested in those who had ecclesiastical descent from Peter.

MARY MAGDALENE

Gnostic writings add another factor to Paul's divergence from the Petrine view. In *The Gospel of Mary*, Mary Magdalene relates a vision she had of the Saviour after his death. In it Jesus describes the nature of the spiritual mysteries, and that the soul of the deceased has to overcome seven limiting powers while journeying to the Aeon, Silence. The gospel continues:

> When Mary had said this, she fell silent, since it was to this point that the Saviour had spoken to her. But Andrew answered and said to the brethren, 'Say what you (wish to) say about what she has said. I at least do not believe that the Saviour said this. For certainly these teachings are strange ideas.'
>
> Peter answered and spoke concerning these same things. He questioned them about the Saviour: 'Did he really speak privately with a woman (and) not openly to us? Are we to turn about and all listen to her? Did he prefer her to us?'
>
> Then Mary wept and said to Peter, 'My brother Peter, what do you think? Do you think I made all this up myself in my heart, or that I am lying about the Saviour?'
>
> Levi answered and said to Peter, 'Peter, you have always been hot-tempered. Now I see you contending against the woman like the adversaries. But if the Saviour made her worthy, who are you indeed to reject her? Surely the Saviour knows her very well. That is why he loved her more than us.[23]

This is not an historical account; rather, it reflects the disagreements that occurred between the divergent orthodox and Gnostic teachings.

While the canonical gospels say little about Mary Magdalene, she is among the first to witness the empty tomb, and in *Matthew* and *John* the first to see the risen Jesus. Despite this, Christianity does not hold Mary Magdalene in high regard, unlike a number of Gnostic texts. The explanation for orthodoxy's lesser respect is unquestionably rooted in the misogynistic attitudes early Christians held towards women (an attitude widespread across Mediterranean cultures). For Gnostics, the feminine principle is equal to that of the male. The earlier-quoted Simonian text explicitly states this:

> Of the universal Aeons there are two shoots, ... the Universal Mind ordering all things, male, and ... the Great Thought, female, producing all things. ... A male-female power like the pre-existing Boundless Power ... existing in oneness.

This fundamental equality of male and female principles led some Gnostic groups to give women equal status in their churches. The Church Fathers, however, did not. Tertullian, taking his lead from Paul (see 1 *Corinthians* 14 34-35) wrote:

> It is not permitted for a woman to speak in the church, nor is it permitted for her to teach, nor to baptise, nor to offer the Eucharist, nor to claim for herself a share in any masculine function—least of all, in priestly office.[24]

On these grounds Tertullian denounced the promenent Gnostic teacher Marcion for appointing women priests and bishops equally with men.

Cultural misogyny is responsible for Mary Magdalene's position being downgraded by the Fathers, and also explains why they emphasised the presence of a prostitute, Helen, in their Magus narrative. Interestingly, Mary and Helen are described in very similar terms. Both were prostitutes, both were saved by a redeemer-figure, and both played a significant role in their redeemer's life.

This commonality leads to fascinating questions. Are Mary

and Helen separate historical individuals? Are they individual manifestations of a single myth? Or are they historical identities who we can only see now through the filter of mythology? If the latter, to what extent does Mary, like Helen, reflect Gnostic mythologising, in which the feminine principle is called The Mother; She of the Left-hand, paired with Christ, him of the Right-hand; Prouneikos or Lustful-one, the Harlot; the Virgin; Consort of the Masculine One; and She who knows the Mysteries of the Elect?

Given our lack of historical information, these questions remain intriguing, but unanswerable.

SIMON MAGUS AND JESUS

Simon Magus's narrative similarly includes details present in Jesus' story. Like Jesus, Simon was associated with John the Baptist; like Jesus, he travelled to Egypt; like Jesus, he was accompanied by a prostitute; like Jesus, he was responsible for acts of magic; and like Jesus, he was a teacher, offering the lost a path to salvation.

What is the relationship between the two? Why do these details from their stories mirror each other so closely? As with Helen and Mary, have both teachers' stories been mythologised? The gospels were written after Simon Magus's death, so did Simon's narrative come first? Did mythologised elements from Simon's story then seep into the gospel narratives? Or do the narrative similarities exist because Simon and Jesus really historically did what is recorded?

These are yet more unanswerable questions. Nonetheless, given the echoes between Simon's and Jesus' stories, we may surmise the Church Fathers viewed the Magus and his teachings as a threat, and responded in a standard human way: they eliminated the competition by deriding Simon as a heretic.

This was not an inevitable decision. The Church Fathers chose it because it suited their purposes in establishing a new religion. But looking back today, we may regret that their choices resulted in valuable contributors to Western spirituality being excluded from our collective cultural memory. Besides Simon Magus, notable absences include Valentinus, Apollonius of Tyana, Marcion, Bardesanes, and three Gnostic women who we only know by name, Marcellina, Flora, and Flavia Sophe. Even more regrettable is that if Gnostic literature had not been destroyed, it could have become part of our cultural heritage, alongside Homeric poetry, Athenian drama, Pre-Socratic, Platonic and Aristotelian philosophy, and Roman literature.

It is too late now to integrate historic Gnostic thought into our world view. Culturally, we have moved on. Gnostic texts and the ideas they present no longer speak to us with the same vivid urgency that inspired their first readers. Nonetheless, the texts that survive conjure for us an era of intense spiritual thirst, when visionaries ignited our forebears' lives with inspiring narratives and vaulting thoughts. That high-mindedness is still needed today.

Simon Magus and his fellow seekers offer us a vision of a spiritualised world that is non-hierarchical, egalitarian and intellectually, emotionally and spiritually aspires to transcend the limitations of our times. That aspect of his message remains highly relevant to us today. The Gnostics profoundly challenged assumptions made about the world in which they lived. May we use their example to continue doing so today.

The Testimony of Simon Magus

I begin with history. I was a pupil once,
long ago, of Yohannes, a hard man
who lived many years in the wilderness,
fasting and praying that he might find God.
Thirty disciples shared that search with him
until his murder by Herod Antipas,
when each chose to go his separate way.
Some died; some gave up; some found another path.
I sought Alexandria's wisdom, to learn
Egyptian philosophy and magic;
that magic is my reputation's source.
Yet I must make a confession.
For the truth is, despite my reputation,
I possess no magical skills at all.
It is true. I am empty of magic.
On what, then, does my reputation rest?
On a lie. Whatever happens works through me,
occurring wholly without my conscious will.
Any strength I have consists in but one skill:
that I can remove myself from myself,
and allow to flow what the powers choose.
That power, compared to which we are nothing,
flows not only through me, but through you all,
through, in truth, the entire manifest world.
As a power it is intangible, because
so subtle and all-transcending; yet by

our lesser awareness it can, in part, be known.
Learn, then, this truth: the world is full of gods.
Greece has Zeus, Persia Ahura Mazdah,
Egypt the ever-present Amen-Ra,
each nation else its own guardian gods
which, through a lesser pantheon, rewards
and punishes those who crave their guidance.
In Judaea here Yahweh fills that function.
And this I say is good, for whether real
or imagined, these gods imbue in worshippers
doubt, that we are of petty significance.
And yet, despite their holy exercises,
this piety is ignorance too; for there
exists another God, incomprehensible,
so deep and vast it is unknown to all.
This God is a power of immeasurable light,
a Fire burning in the midst of Silence,
the ultimate mover of earthly existence,
yet inaccessible to the earthly senses.
So great is this Fire, so intense its being,
that none can see it directly; the shock
would obliterate their shuddering soul.
Thus there exists a spiritual order
whereby what we cannot bear naked descends
through an intermediate hierarchy,
to end clothed in the flesh of suns and stars,
whose physical light but reflects that Fire
which filters down from the regions above.
Yet if Fire above descended below,
so a path exists from the sensory
creation back to the spiritual source,
and this fleshly encasement is not our end,
but a springboard rather from which we may,

in knowledge, rebound to that from which we came.
Only then does the Unknown God manifest,
and the Hidden Fire stand revealed.
Knowing that Fire, to the degree permitted,
is the sole purpose of all our knowing;
that is the miracle we have the power to live.
Understand, this Fire's nature is double,
one part manifest, the other concealed.
To fully perceive Fire's doubleness,
picture a great Tree grown from a single Root.
This Root is as a hidden Treasure House,
the great Tree its manifest projection,
which is wholly flesh, and burns the savage
desiring way of all sensory forms,
devoured in what it's nourished by.
But Fire's purpose is not futile, projecting
to destroy; the Tree grows fine fruit also,
and if, by perspicacious application,
this fruit perfects its imaging and becomes
what it is, it is not destroyed by flame,
but is transported to the Treasure House
where, completed, it resides forever.
We are that fruit, our task to manifest
what in us else must remain concealed.
And when our imaging is perfected,
and to the Treasure House we are returned,
we become harmonious to the Root,
and our concealed Fire becomes Boundless Power,
the great Father which presides over all.
Thus though we start dull earth, commodious
to the powers which rule this earthly sphere,
within we are Fire, with rising hope

to surpass even heaven's angels
and reach that Power which stands above all.
This is our end, for this task are we born:
to start lost in earth, but end pure Fire.

References

End notes

1   *Simon Magus* p 24, and *The Gnostic Gospels* (originally pub-
     lished 1979, here London: Phoenix Books, 2006), p 69.
2   See Elaine Pagels' account of this process in *Beyond Belief:*
     The Secret Gospel of Thomas (NY: Vintage Books, 2003).
3   All Bible quotations are from *The Jerusalem Bible*, Alexander
     Jones (Ed.), (London: Darton, Longman & Todd, 1966).
4   *The Gospel According to Thomas*, logion 3, p 118 This gospel
     exists in multiple translations. Unless stated otherwise, all
     Gnostic texts quoted here are from *The Nag Hammadi Li-*
     brary: In English (NHL), translated by Members of the Coptic
     Gnostic Library Project of the Institute for Antiquity and
     Christianity directed by James M. Robinson (San Francisco:
     Harper & Row, 1981).
5   *The Second Treatise of the Great Seth*, NHL, pp 333-334.
6   Pagels, *The Gnostic Gospels*, pp 50, 64.
7   G.R.S. Mead, *Fragments of a Faith Forgotten* (London: Theo-
     sophical Publishing Society: 1900/1906) p 223. The 1906 edi-
     tion is reproduced on-line by the Gnostic Society Library,
     with the original pagination used here: http://www.gnosis.
     org/library/grs-mead/fragments_faith_forgotten/index.htm
8   Pagels, *The Gnostic Gospels*, p 48.
9   From the *Govishn Ig Griv Zindag*, in *The Other Bible*, Wallis
     Barnstone (editor), (SF: Harper & Row, 1984), p 315. The ex-
     cerpt is reproduced from a translation by Jes P. Asmussen,
     Manichean Literature (NY: Scholars Facsimiles and Reprints,
     1976), p 81.

10   *The Gospel of Thomas*, logion 108, NHL, p 129.

11   Mead, *Simon Magus*, p 8.

12   Mead, *Fragments of a Faith Forgotten*, pp 589-590.

13   The earliest extent biography, *Life of Apollonius*, was written over 120 years after his death by Philostratus. Apollonius himself wrote several books, and was referenced—reverently—by numerous early writers. None of his or their texts survived the destruction of pagan literature ordered by Justinian and Pope Gregory in the sixth century. Mead has marshalled all available resources to construct a biography of Apollonius. His book is still in print and on-line via the Gnostic Society Library. First century concepts of magic and the representation of sages as magicians have been fascinatingly explored by Morton Smith in his study, *Jesus the Magician* (1978).

14   Mead, *Simon Magus*, pp 32-33.

15   Ibid, p 22.

16   Ibid, pp 9-10.

17   *The Exegesis on the Soul*, NHL pp 180-181.

18   Mead, *Simon Magus*, pp 13, 21-22.

19   For a comparison with Hermetic thought see Brian P. Copenhaver, *Hermetica* (Cambridge University Press, 1992). For a discussion of dating see p 95. Copenhaver also extensively discusses connections of Gnostic and Hermetic thought.

20   Mead, *Fragments of a Faith Forgotten*, p 175.

21   Mead, *Simon Magus*, p 27.

22   Mead, *Fragments*, p 166.

23   *The Gospel of Mary*, NHL, p 473.

24   Quoted in Pagels, *The Gnostic Gospels*, p 81.

Further reading

All texts related to Simon Magus are collected in G.R.S. Mead's *Simon Magus* (1892). In the following end notes I reference the reprint of the 1906 reprint. This text is available on-line. Only one other book since Mead has examined the historical Simon Magus. *Son of Perdition: The Magic and Hubris of Simon Magus* by M.R. Osbourne (2022), interestingly re-evaluates the Magus' reputation, focusing on his magical practice.

I wish to draw attention to the value of G.R.S. Mead's writings on Gnosticism, early Christianity and Western esoteric traditions. Today Mead is not cited by academics due to his work being judged 'tainted' by his association with Theosophy. Nonetheless, his knowledge of the most arcane writings and ideas of the Classical and early Christian eras is not matched by any modern scholars. While he wrote prior to the discoveries of the Nag Hammadi codexes, and much has been learned since then, Mead drew on the work of leading European scholars, much of whose research remains relevant today. Mead was also the first to translate Gnostic works into English—his translation and commentaries on *Pistis Sophia* haven't been bettered. His work was certainly appreciated: Carl Jung personally visited Mead to thank him for his writing on the Gnostics.

All Mead's books are available free to read on-line: http://www.gnosis.org/library/grs-mead/mead_index.htm

To update Mead, a useful place to start is *The Gnostic Gospels* (1979) by Elaine Pagels. Pagels is an academic whose specialty is early Christianity, but her books are aimed at non-specialists.

The Gnostic Gospels establishes the historical and religious background, recounts the Nag Hammadi discoveries, and considers the implications. In *Beyond Belief: The Secret Gospel of Thomas* (2022), Pagels examines the historical process by which the Church Fathers created and suppressed heresies. She doesn't discuss Simon Magus, but Beyond Belief offers a much more detailed consideration of the Fathers' thinking and actions.

For an overview of historical Gnosticism, David Brakke's *The Gnostics: Myth, Ritual, and Diversity in Early Christianity* (2012) is academic but engaging. Tobias Churton is not an academic but draws on scholarly sources. His *Gnostic Philosophy: From Ancient Persia to Modern Times* (2005) examines the impact of Gnostic thought on Western culture. Despite the Catholic Church's suppression, eruptions of Gnostic thinking are surprisingly widespread.

Numerous translations of Gnostic texts have been published. *The Other Bible*, edited by Willis Barnstone, presents numerous early Jewish and Gnostic texts, including Hermetica and Christian apocrypha. This and similar collections show the richness and diversity of non-canonical writing dating to the early Christian period.

To the reader

Small presses rely on the support of readers to tell others about the books they enjoy. To support this book and its author, we ask you to consider placing a review on the site where you bought it. Others in the Classics of World Mysticism series:

Interpretations of Desire
Mystical love poems by the Sufi Master Ibn 'Arabi

Keith Hill's artful and beautiful renditions will bring Ibn 'Arabi's neglected masterpiece to a new readership. —Nile Green, author of *Sufism: A Global History*

In 1201, Shaykh Muhyiddin Ibn 'Arabi arrived in Mecca. Among the many people who impressed him one drew his attention above all others: Nizám, the daughter of a prominent religious teacher. As Beatrice did for Dante, Nizám soon inspired a sequence of love poems that are Ibn 'Arabi's poetic masterpiece, *Tarjumán al-Aswáq* (*The Interpreter of Desire*).

Muhyiddin Ibn 'Arabi was known as Shaykh al-Akbar (the Greatest Shaykh), a title given him due to his profound knowledge as a mystic, theologian, philosopher and legalist. Scholars are devoting much labour to translating and interpreting Ibn 'Arabi's voluminous prose writings, but his poetry remains little known by Western readers compared to Rumi, Attar and Hafiz.

This collection reveals that with his intense feeling, vivid imagery, and the playful way he reworked the conventions of Bedouin desert poetry, Ibn 'Arabi wrote poems that deserve to be placed alongside the best of his illustrious Sufi compatriots.

Psalms of Exile and Return

In a time that seems spiritually dry for so many, this book of psalms is water in the desert. They challenge, terrify, comfort, and call us to a deep humanity. —Allan Jones, Dean Emeritus, Grace Cathedral, San Francisco

In 587 BCE, King Zedekiah of Judah led his people in rebellion against Babylonian rule. Nebuchadnezzar responded mercilessly. His army sacked Jerusalem, destroyed the Temple, and deported thousands to Babylon. These psalms are written from the perspective of one of those exiles. They express his growing unhappiness with life as a slave, his despairing cries for help to his Lord, and his eventual escape into the wilderness. After much struggle he is reunited with his lost beloved, and together they reach Jerusalem.

Inspired by the impassioned Jewish prophets and poets, and in harmony with the Jewish healing tradition of tikkun olam, these poems recount seekers' spiritual journey as they strive to transcend everyday life, enter their own hurt heart, heal its pain, and release the wisdom that exists there. It is the story of exiles who, lost and despairing, rediscover themselves in joy.

I Cannot Live Without You
Selected Poems of Mirabai and Kabir

It's been an eternity since I was hungry for God's pure essence. I Cannot Live Without You reignites a deep passion to see the face of God, even knowing that God has no face. This book will renew your hunger for your sacred flame. —Judith Hoch PhD, author of *Prophecy By the River*

Wild and passionate, Mirabai is India's greatest poet of devotion and love. Married at a young age, after her husband's premature death she dedicated her life to worshipping the flute-playing Krishna. It was a decision that led her parents-in-law to evict her from their home. Mirabai spent the rest of her life travelling from village to village, singing and dancing to celebrate her love of Krishna. The rapturous lyrics she wrote enthralled worshippers then and continue to be sung in India today.

Kabir was a controversial figure. An illiterate weaver, he celebrated both Indian and Muslim spirituality, while criticising each religion's blinkered believers. Yet his straight talking, his wit, and the continued relevance of his insights, ensure his often knotty poems still resonate powerfully with contemporary readers.

These engaging versions will delight readers new to the work of two of India's greatest mystical poets, and surprise those already familiar with their playful profundity.

The Bhagavad Gita
A new poetic translation

An enthralling new rendering ... balances spiritual insight, poetic power and philosophic accuracy. —Peter Calvert, *The Kosmic Web*

On the battlefield of life, desiring to do our best, how should we act? Which values should we live by? What metaphysical outlook best explains what happens to us? How do we express our spiritual nature? And how can we stay spiritually focused in the whirl of daily activity?

Arjuna's searching questions, asked on the brink of a war he is loathe to fight, and Krishna's profound answers, spoken in his chariot as they survey the battlefield on which thousands will soon die, offer timeless insights into the difficulties and wonders of human existence, making the *Bhagavad Gita* one of the great works of world spirituality.

Originally written in poetry, but commonly translated into English in prose, this version balances the need to present the *Bhagavad Gita's* profound concepts precisely while reproducing the original's dramatic and poetic power. This translation is especially successful in capturing the *Bhagavad Gita's* shifts of tone, moving from vivid descriptions of the battlefield, to the precise reasoning of Krishna's advice to Arjuna, to the sublime visionary intensity of Krishna as cosmic being. Endnotes and a glossary help readers unfamiliar with Indian culture understand the poem's mythological and philosophic references.